The [illegible] Ch[illegible]mas of a Cat Lady

To Anna

Enjoy the Kitten Chaos!

Editor: Sofia Artola Diaz
Proofreader: Stephanie Savu / Happily Booked PR
Beta Reader: Nina Harris

PA Support: Happily Booked PR & Nina Harris

Contents

Content Warning

This book contains all of the following:

> Strong language & scenes of sexual nature

> Cheating

If any of this serves as a trigger for you, please decide if this is the book for you.

Finally, the book is set in England and British English spelling is used throughout. That means a lot of times you'll find an "S" where you may expect a "Z". And our ass has an extra Rrrrr to it ;-). Also get ready to learn new words like knobhead and numpty and a bit about Britain's weird history (Bonfire Night is real and I love it!)

Dedication

Dedicated to the cats who think Christmas trees are climbing frames.
And to the humans who love them anyway.

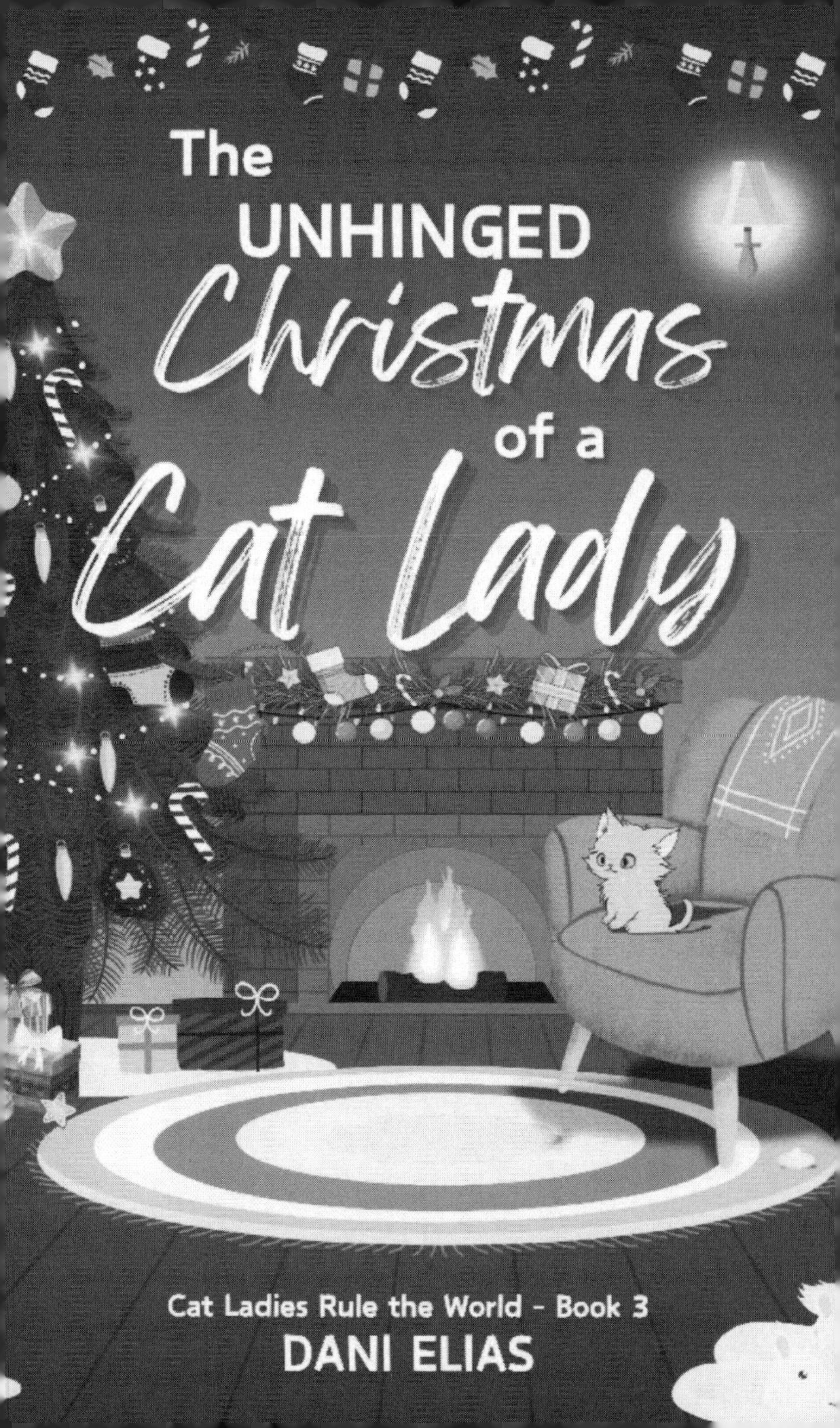
The
UNHINGED
Christmas
of a
Cat Lady
Cat Ladies Rule the World - Book 3
DANI ELIAS

Baby, It's Cold Inside

Prologue

August

Miranda

The train reeks of sweat and crisps and something vaguely chemical no one wants to identify. I shift in my seat, but the back of my legs is stuck, and every movement threatens to peel away a layer of skin. The fan above me rattles pointlessly. It's too hot to breathe properly, never mind travel halfway up the country.

Happy birthday to me. Somehow, I thought forty-two might feel different. Less sticky.

I wasn't supposed to be on a train from Cornwall to London. But then the flowers arrived just after breakfast, hand-delivered to Irene's front step in a box big enough to qualify as furniture. White roses, those droopy purple things florists get excited about, and eucalyptus that smelled like the inside of a fancy spa. The card was tucked in the middle, properly written out in Sim-Sim's handwriting.

I wish I could be with you today.
You're the best thing that ever happened
to me. Happy birthday, my love.
Sim-Sim x

I read it twice. We've never been the note-writing type. Not the hearts-and-roses couple. There were no speeches about fate or soulmates, no violins tucked into corners. We got married because we had a seven-year-old and his family wouldn't stop banging on about it.

They'd been at us for years. "Make it official," "Think of SJ," "It's just the right thing to do." I lost count of how many times Irene said, "It's not about tradition, it's about stability for your son." In the end, we gave in.

The cake was excellent. SJ wore his first proper suit and danced until he passed out on a pile of coats. But if it had just been up to me, I'm not sure we'd have bothered. We already lived together, raised a child together. The vows felt more like confirming what we were already doing, but in front of two hundred and twenty witnesses and a photographer who kept calling me "Mrs G" like I was someone's deputy headmistress.

Since then, we've carried on the way we always have. Sim-Sim working twelve-hour days, me handling everything else. He's good at what he does. The firm's doubled in size since the wedding a year and a half ago. But with it came the stress and the lack of family time.

So when he said he couldn't come to Cornwall for our summer holidays, I didn't push. He had a case to sort. SJ and I packed up and left him to it.

And then this morning, the flowers arrived. And the note. And Irene, watching me the way only a mother-in-law can, said firmly, "Go."

So I did.

I shift again. Nothing helps. The seat's too hot, the carriage too loud, and my arse feels laminated.

Home's still a few hours away. Sim-Sim won't be expecting me. Won't be expecting much of anything, actually. I can't even remember when we did anything remotely romantic or had sex.

That stupid red underwear's still in the top drawer. The one Amelia talked me into buying back in March. We were supposed to be shopping for a birthday present for Lizzie and somehow ended up in a shop full of silk and straps and lighting designed to make everything look like a good idea.

She handed it to me without saying much. Just a little nod and a weirdly firm look, as if I was overdue some kind of awakening. I snorted and said she'd been spending too much time with Ben.

She went pink, obviously. She always does. None of us expected quiet, cardigan-wearing Amelia, the epitome of a cat lady, to end up in a full-blown pleasure-dom-arrangement, but here we are. She never talks about it, not really—just stammers and changes the subject which only makes it funnier, if we're honest. I know she is happy in her relationship, more than happy, and as her friend I couldn't hope for more. But secretly I was probably a little jealous, because I don't think Sim-Sim and I were ever quite where Amelia and Ben are. We are more practical, more pragmatic.

But maybe that needs to change. I'll be home tonight. With him. Maybe I'll wear it... the little red thing.

Maybe he'll remember why he married me.

Or maybe I'll end up sitting on the sofa in it, eating crisps and waiting for the washing machine to finish.

Could go either way.

The flat's silent when I get in.

Cold air hits me the second I open the door and I nearly moan out loud. Air conditioning's going full tilt, bless it. We are probably the envy of most British people—a home with a rare air condition. That's what Sim-Sim's success got us. A swanky flat in Battersea with all the amenities your heart could ask for.

After slipping off my shoes, I drop my bag by the bench in the hall, and glance around. Sim-Sim's keys aren't in the tray, which means I've beaten him home. *Perfect.*

I head for the bedroom, toes sinking into the thick carpet, breathing easier already.

The door's ajar. Sunlight's spilling in making me squint. For one glorious second, I think about a shower, a glass of wine, maybe even shaving my legs.

Then I see it.

Her.

On her knees.

Pigtails. Tartan mini-skirt. Shirt tied under her chest like some sort of budget Britney cosplay. She's bobbing up and down with real enthusiasm, as if she's auditioning for a scholarship.

Sim-Sim's got his head tipped back, shirt half-off, tie dangling like he's just got home from an exhausting day at the office and now this is the reward. He moans.

"You're such a good baby girl for daddy."

For a moment I honestly think I've walked into someone else's flat. I look at the rug. It's ours. The curtains, the painting over the bed—ours. That is, in fact, my husband. Getting sucked off by a woman more than a decade younger than me.

I don't move. I don't utter a sound. My brain is still rebooting.

Daddy.

What the fuck? Is that what he is into?

Three seconds. Maybe four. Long enough to really take it in. The way her pleats swing. The way his hand is on her head guiding her until she makes a gagging noise... a noise that seems to really get him going.

Happy fucking birthday to me.

When I step into the room, they both freeze. She's halfway to standing, mouth slightly open, pigtails and tartan skirt doing her no favours. He's just standing there, eyes wide, pure panic on his face, trousers around his ankles and a rapidly softening dick—never a great sight if I may say so.

"Miranda—"

"Oh, do shut up," I stop him. "I'd hate to interrupt whatever GCSE roleplay this is."

The woman tucks on the hem of her skirt but she won't meet my eyes. *Good.*

I stare down Sim-Sim. It feels like this is the only power I have left: confronting this head on.

"I got the flowers," I say. "Lovely arrangement, really tasteful. Almost made me think you gave a fuck."

He winces.

"And the note. Very touching. Really. Especially the part about me being the best thing that ever happened to you. I must admit, I didn't realise you were measuring that against a blowjob from someone who still gets ID'd for paracetamol."

She mumbles something. I hold up a hand.

"No. Don't. You don't need to explain. I'm not here to scold you. I'm here because it's my birthday, and I thought my *husband* would love for me to pop by given that his card said he wished I could be with him. I thought maybe I can do something nice for him. My mistake to assume he wouldn't arrange for someone else to give him *that*."

He takes a breath like he's about to go for sympathy. I shake my head.

"I left SJ in Cornwall. I sat on a train for five hours next to a man eating egg salad out of Tupperware. I was going to wear that red underwear I bought for a special occasion. My marriage falling apart wasn't quite the special occasion I had in mind."

He still says nothing. Nothing.

I let the silence stretch.

"Well," I say. "You've certainly made this birthday one to remember."

Then I turn on my heel.

"I'm going to shower. When I come back out, I expect her to be gone. And you to decide whether you're going to come clean or keep lying through your teeth until the bitter end. Either way, this is over."

I don't slam the door; he doesn't deserve my anger.

1

Silent Night, Mediator Fright

November – Present time

Miranda

The mediator's office smells faintly of damp carpet and nerves. There's a bowl of dusty boiled sweets on the table and a fake orchid wilting in the corner. Someone's tried very hard to make the place feel calm. It hasn't worked.

Sim-Sim's already here. He stands when I walk in, which is pointless but typical. His lawyer's beside him—a lean man in a navy suit with expensive glasses and the air of someone who has made a fortune out of the misery of others.

Claire, the mediator, offers a warm, over-rehearsed smile and introduces everyone, even though we've all met before. Maybe it's for show. Maybe it's protocol. Or maybe she just can't tell we'd all rather be anywhere else.

On my side of the table is Renata. My solicitor. Kind, efficient, sharp as a bread knife. She doesn't do small talk, which I appreciate. She gives me a quiet nod as I settle into my seat.

Claire launches into her usual script. Fairness. Neutrality. Constructive dialogue. Her tone is soft, calm, the voice of a woman who's probably guided more couples into polite endings than she cares to remember.

Sim-Sim doesn't say anything. He keeps his hands clasped together in front of him. His lawyer whispers something in his ear, and he nods.

He didn't want the divorce. Still doesn't. He said it was one mistake. One stupid, meaningless, porn-grade decision that "meant nothing."

Right. Once a cheater, always a cheater. I just couldn't see a way back.

Renata turns the page.

"We need to address the housing situation," she says. "Miranda is currently living in the Battersea property, which remains the primary residence for both her and SJ. She's in the guest room. It's a temporary arrangement, but it would be disruptive to move her and the child."

Sim-Sim's lawyer Giles clears his throat. "To clarify, the Battersea flat is owned solely by Mr Gordon. It was purchased before the marriage and is not considered a joint marital asset."

"I'm aware," Renata replies, calm. "We're not disputing ownership. We're talking about continuity and security for the child."

"Simon Junior," Giles says, and I nearly roll my eyes into another tax bracket.

"Simon Junior Junior," I correct him, deadpan. "Or SJ, as literally everyone calls him."

Giles gives a tight little smile.

"We've agreed Mr Gordon covers SJ's expenses," Giles continues. "School fees, clothing, travel. There's no dispute there. He'll provide generously."

Renata doesn't blink. "But no spousal maintenance. Despite the fact that Miranda paused her career at the birth of their son, in agreement with Mr Gordon, and has not been in full-time employment since."

"She's capable of working," Giles says. "There's no physical or medical barrier. Or, of course, she could remain in the marriage. That option is still open."

I laugh. Just once, sharp and humourless.

"Oh, is it? How generous. I get a choice—poverty or forgiveness."

Sim-Sim finally speaks. "It's not about punishment, Miranda. I made a mistake."

"So you've said."

Claire shifts slightly in her chair. Renata stays completely still.

"You offered to cover everything for SJ," I continue. "That's fine. But I'm not just the woman who made him packed lunches for eight years. I gave up my job. My pension. My independence. Because we agreed that was what was best for the family. Your words."

"And now you want me to keep paying you," Sim-Sim says. "What for? To prove I'm sorry?"

"No," I say. "Because I did the work. You built a business. I built a life around it. I won't apologise for expecting that to count for something."

He looks down at the table.

Claire clears her throat gently. "Would you both like a short break?"

"No," I say, voice flat. "We're not done yet."

Giles leans forward, folding his hands in that lawyerly way that signals *this part isn't up for discussion.*

"My client is clear," he says. "He is not prepared to pay spousal maintenance. That is non-negotiable."

I nod, slowly. "Of course. Heaven forbid I drain the hedge fund."

Renata places a calming hand on her notes, but says nothing.

Giles continues. "Mr Gordon has offered to contribute fifty percent of any rent Miranda pays going forward, which is generous and ensures SJ's housing is secure. He's also willing to cover the cost of any childcare she requires while returning to work. This is not about withholding support. This is about creating fair, sustainable terms."

"Fair," I say. "Yes, because nothing says fairness like your ex-husband subsidising a shoebox while you try to convince someone to hire you after nearly a decade out of the workforce. Very empowering."

Sim-Sim glances at me, jaw tense.

"You said you wanted to be free of me," he says quietly.

"No, I said I wanted respect," I snap. "But clearly that comes out of a different budget."

The room goes still for a second too long.

Claire straightens her posture, smoothing her expression into something neutral. "Let me remind both parties," she says, her voice still soft but firmer now, "that if we cannot reach an agreement on these terms, the case will have to proceed to family court."

She lets that sit.

"That will involve significant delays. Possibly months. You'll both lose control of the outcome, and any judge will prioritise the welfare of the child above all else. So I would encourage you to consider whether continued negotiation might be preferable to formal proceedings."

Renata turns to me.

Just a glance. Calm. But I know that look.

It's the one that says, *You can push this if you want, but it's a risk. A judge might not side with you. And if it goes the wrong way, you could end up with even less.*

Less support. Less say. Less everything.

Because the law doesn't care that I spent the last eight years raising a child while Sim Sim doubled his company's assets. It cares that I'm fit, healthy, and technically employable. It cares that there's no violence, no addiction, no chaos. Just a marriage quietly dismantled by arrogance and lust.

Sim-Sim, to his credit—or maybe just his advantage—says nothing.

He knows Renata's look too.

I tap my fingers on the table, once, then stop.

"Fine," I say.

It comes out quieter than I mean it to.

I clear my throat and try again.

"Fine," sharper this time. "I'll take the half rent. I'll take the childcare. And I'll find a job."

No one says anything. Not even Claire.

I look across the table at Sim-Sim.

"You win."

He shakes his head slightly. "It's not about winning, Miranda."

"No," I say, "of course not. This is just the prize you get for being consistently disappointing."

Claire clears her throat.

"Shall we move on to the next item?" she says gently.

Renata nods. She's already turning the page.

I sit back and breathe through my nose. I don't blink. I don't cry. And I sure as hell don't give Sim-Sim the satisfaction of looking broken.

But in the pit of my stomach, something folds in on itself.

It's late afternoon by the time I get to Little Hadlow. The sun's already losing its confidence and the air smells faintly of woodsmoke and wet leaves. November is doing its best to look poetic while everyone quietly freezes to death.

I couldn't face going back to the flat.

Not after that.

Sim-Sim had the nerve to look relieved when I told him I'd be out for the evening. Said he'd do a father–son dinner. Pizza and Mario Kart, I expect. Bonding time, he called it.

I nodded, packed a bag, and left before I started shouting in front of SJ.

Now I'm standing on Amelia and Ben's doorstep, bag in hand, eyes scratchy with exhaustion and fury I haven't quite finished processing.

I press the doorbell.

Nothing.

I try again. A longer press.

Still nothing.

I glance through the frosted glass. No movement. Just a warm hallway and the faint outline of someone's coat on the hook.

I press it a third time, this time with less patience.

The door swings open.

Ben. Shirt halfway over his head, bare legs, boxers. Tartan, obviously.

His face shifts the second he sees me.

I step forward. The tears hit before I even open my mouth.

No warning. Just full-body crying. Heat behind my eyes, throat locked, everything crumpling at once.

I don't give him a chance to say anything. I just walk straight past him into the house where I drop my bag on the wooden floor.

Smutty appears from the living room, tail swishing, expression deeply unimpressed. He pauses in the doorway, clocks it's me, then vanishes again without fanfare.

Ben closes the door. "Bloody hell, Miranda," he says softly behind me. "What's happened?"

I shake my head, uselessly. Hands braced on my knees. Breath dragging in like I've run a mile uphill in heels.

Everything's shaking—or I am. Hard to tell.

"Where's Amelia?" I manage, voice rough.

Ben grins, that familiar, lopsided one. "Bedroom. I'll get her."

He turns.

And that's when it hits me.

The boxers. The flushed grin. The slow door. Of course they were.

"Oh god," I mutter. "Ben."

He stops on the first step, glancing back over his shoulder.

"I'm so sorry," I say, straightening up, wiping my face with the back of my hand. "I didn't think. I should've texted. I've just—fuck. I didn't mean to barge in on—whatever—"

He waves a hand, still smiling, but softer now.

"Don't be daft. You're always welcome. Even mid-orgasm."

That gets a laugh out of me. Croaky. Stupid. But real.

"Give us a sec. I'll go grab her."

He pads up the staircase, still entirely too casual in his boxers. The floor creaks faintly overhead, then a door opens. Muffled voices. Amelia's, soft and surprised.

I lean back against the wall. The house smells of fabric softener and wood polish. There's a jumper hung on the banister and a pair of trainers kicked off by the coat rack. Ordinary things. Warm things.

This is what a home should feel like.

The stairs creak again.

Amelia appears, cheeks flushed, hair slightly mussed, fully dressed in yoga pants and an oversized T-shirt that reads *Cat Ladies Rule the World* in faded lettering.

She doesn't say a word. Just walks straight up to me and wraps me in her arms.

She's warm. Solid. Comfort in human form. No pressure, no questions—just the steady weight of someone who knows exactly how to hold a person together.

I fold into her. Breathe in that faint scent of lemon and let myself cry.

Behind her, Ben comes back down the stairs, now in jeans and a grey T-shirt. Smutty winds between his ankles and lets himself be scooped up like a prince accepting tribute. He curls against Ben's chest, purring happily.

Ben glances at us and nods. "I'll put the kettle on."

2

Rockin' Around the Bonfire

Miranda

The kitchen is quiet, warm, familiar. A lamp glows in the corner. The mugs are already out, the kettle halfway through boiling. The kind of normality I haven't felt in weeks.

I slide onto a stool at the island. Amelia sits across from me, Ben beside her, his hand resting lightly on her lower back.

"I'm so bloody tired," I say quietly. "I didn't realise how much until now."

Amelia leans in. "What happened?"

I stare at the countertop for a moment.

"The divorce's final. Signed today. I didn't even look at him when I did it."

Amelia's lips press into a hard line.

"He's not paying me anything," I continue. "Just SJ's costs. No maintenance. Half my rent for SJ's sake and, apparently, as a favour. And he'll cover childcare so I can get a job. Out of the kindness of his heart."

Ben swears under his breath.

Amelia sits back slightly. "That's disgusting."

I let out a dry, bitter laugh. "It's perfectly legal. Renata gave me the look—you know, the one that says, *We can fight this, but you'll lose*. The courts don't care that I raised our son while he doubled the company's net worth and stuck his dick wherever it suited him. They see someone fit and educated and say, 'Well, back to work with you.'"

"He cheated on you," Amelia says, cheeks flushed. "And now he gets to come out of it with his flat, his business, his reputation, and you get... what? A pat on the head and half the rent?"

"Pretty much," I say. "But don't worry: the offer to go back to him to 'save our marriage' still stands. Apparently, he still thinks that's a possibility."

Amelia's jaw actually drops. "You're joking."

"I wish I was. He said I could stay. In the guest room. To work things out."

Ben lets out a low, disgusted breath. "Jeez."

I grip the edge of the counter.

"I gave up everything for that marriage," I say. "My work. My financial independence. My bloody sanity, most days. And now I get to start over with no savings, and a son who has no idea that his father thinks monogamy is optional."

My voice cracks at the end. Not loud. But enough.

Amelia gets up, walks around the island, and wraps her arms around me again. I press my forehead to her shoulder. The tears don't come this time, but I wish they would. It would be easier than this bone-deep, pulsing fury that doesn't seem to go anywhere.

Behind us, the kettle clicks off.

Ben sets down a fresh mug and leans against the counter, arms crossed, watching us for a beat. "What you need tonight is a girls' evening."

I lift my head, eyes red but dry. "What I need is a bottle of wine and a flame-thrower."

"Sure," he says, unbothered. "We can do both. But first—come with us to the bonfire."

I blink at him. "What bonfire?"

Ben gives me a look. "It's the fifth of November."

Guy Fawkes Night. Can't believe I forgot. Then again, I forgot what day it was until Renata handed me the final agreement and said *You're free* in that voice lawyers use when they mean *You've been mugged politely*.

"It's the football club's do," he adds. "Out on the pitch. Burgers, cider, small children with glow sticks. The others are all going as well."

Amelia nods. "They'll want to see you. And you don't have to say anything. Just turn up. Let us feed you and take care of you."

Ben grins. "You could burn an effigy of Sim-Sim. Really lean into the theme."

Amelia raises her eyebrows. "I've got paper and string. We can knock one together. Just say the word."

That gets a real laugh out of me. Croaky, but proper.

"I'd need at least three heads to get the proportions right," I mutter.

Ben lifts his mug. "To creative vengeance."

Amelia clinks hers against his. I just shake my head and sip my tea, a flicker of warmth settling somewhere in my chest.

What would I do without my friends?

We're all standing on the village green, coats zipped up, hands wrapped around paper cups of something hot and questionably alcoholic. The bonfire crackles ahead, flames punching heat into the cold air, smoke drifting in soft clouds across the pitch.

Above us, fireworks burst into bloom. Red. Gold. Electric white. The kind that fizz before they fall. Someone near the front whistles. A small child squeals with delight.

Over the stadium speaker, the moderator reads in full theatre voice:

"Remember, remember, the fifth of November, Gunpowder, treason and plot..."

I've heard it every year of my life. This time, it feels oddly reassuring. The rhythm of it. The predictability. A poem about burning things down and carrying on.

Around me, my friends huddle close in pairs.

Ben and Amelia, arms linked, smiling quietly. Lizzie and Coop, sharing a drink and a scarf. Bri, tucked under Omar's coat. Fi laughing at something George whispers in her ear.

It's not jealousy. Not even longing. Just loneliness. A quiet awareness of being the only one without someone's hand in mine. The only one with no one to lean into when the cold starts to creep in.

I'm not thinking about Sim-Sim.

It's not him I'm missing... at all.

Just the warmth. The *us-ness*. The thing I thought I had.

I sip the drink. It's sweet, spiced, sharp at the back of the throat.

I breathe in smoke and fireworks and the comfort of standing close to people who still see me.

And that, for now, will have to be enough.

The last of the fireworks fizzles out in a crackle of white sparks, the kind that hang in the sky like someone forgot to turn the stars off.

People start to drift. Boots crunching on damp grass. Children herded. The smell of smoke clings to everything.

We begin the slow shuffle back toward Ben and Amelia's. Fi is already plotting hot chocolate logistics. Omar's explaining, very seriously, why he should never be trusted with pyrotechnics.

As we cross the edge of the green, someone jogs past us—tall, lean, with a little girl tucked on his hip. She's about five, dark hair in two lopsided plaits, face half-buried in the collar of his jacket. She's holding onto a half-eaten toffee apple like it's a state treasure.

"Jasper!" Coop calls, waving. "Alright, mate?"

The man lifts a hand in greeting, doesn't break stride. The girl yawns against his shoulder.

Lizzie watches them pass, then leans into Coop. "Who was that?"

"Jasper," he says. "Plays on the team with us. You've met him, haven't you?"

She shakes her head, but doesn't press.

Amelia suddenly huffs. "My toes are actual ice cubes. If we don't speed up, I'm sawing them off in the hallway."

That gets us moving. We pick up the pace, crunching over gravel and leaves, hands jammed in pockets, everyone a bit colder now the fireworks are done.

Ben unlocks the door, lets us all in, and immediately heads for the speakers in the corner of the living room. Within seconds, something upbeat and retro fills the house—the kind of playlist that promises both familiarity and at least two singalongs later.

The snacks come out in chaotic, communal waves—mini pizzas shoved in the oven, sausage rolls warming in a tray, a mountain of scotch eggs, at least two salads that no one will touch until guilt kicks in. Someone finds crisps. Someone else opens another bottle of wine.

I end up chopping cherry tomatoes with Bri while Fi wrestles with a clingfilm-covered quiche and yells at Ben for using the wrong knife for cheese.

"Where's Robbie tonight?" I ask Fi. She and George already have two grown-up children, and just when Fi thought she was about to earn her freedom and start browsing holiday brochures, along came Robbie, the surprise baby-shaped plot twist.

"Claire and her boyfriend are down from uni," Fi says. "She offered to take him to Lewes for the big bonfire... playing big sister for the day, which means George and I get a sort-of date night." She grins and plants a kiss on George's lips. Honestly, they're so happy together it's like they're trying for another surprise baby.

Smutty slinks across the counter like a feline burglar, tail flicking with intention.

"Oi!" Amelia snaps, swatting at him with a tea towel. "Not tonight, Furball."

Smutty blinks at her, absolutely unrepentant, then makes a slow, sulky exit—only to immediately double back toward the sausage rolls the moment her back's turned.

There's laughter. Real laughter. Tired, a bit wine-fuelled, but honest.

And for the first time in what feels like weeks, I feel like a person again—not a wife, or an ex-wife, or a woman stuck between court papers and cardboard boxes. Just me.

We're all around the kitchen table now, plates cluttered with crumbs and half-eaten sausage rolls, wine glasses catching the warm overhead light. The food's taken the edge off, but the ache behind my eyes still simmers.

Omar puts down his fork and says, "Right. I've just thought of something."

"Dangerous," Bri murmurs, not looking up.

"No, listen. That bloke we passed earlier on the green—with the little girl? Jasper."

There are a few vague nods.

"He's got this big place just a few roads over," Omar goes on. "It's a big house but it also has a self-contained flat attached... like a proper annexe. Own entrance, kitchen, all of it."

I squint at him, half-suspicious. "And?"

"You should move in," he says simply. "It's empty."

I blink. "Wait, what?"

"He bought the place for the house itself," Omar explains. "The flat was just part of the deal. He doesn't use it. It's just sitting there."

Lizzie's already grinning. "You could live here! SJ would love it. The space, the garden, all the kids around."

"His school's in London," I remind them. "I can't just uproot him."

Ben, casually reaching for his phone, says, "Sim-Sim's paying for transport. It's in the divorce agreement."

"Sure, but—"

"It doesn't say from where," Ben adds. "And let's be honest, getting across half of London can take longer than a train from here."

I open my mouth, ready to protest, and promptly close it again.

He's not wrong.

Ben's already standing. "Let's just see if it's an option."

"Wait—are you calling him now?"

"Yes."

"Ben—!"

Too late. He steps into the hallway to make the call that could change my life... yet again.

There's a beat of silence.

Then Coop says, "Jasper doesn't need the money. I don't think he was planning to rent it out. But if someone were to ask, I'd bet he'd say yes. Especially if Ben puts the charm on."

I glance around at the circle of eager, determined faces.

And realise I'm the only one who hasn't agreed to this plan yet.

3

Guy Fox Is Coming to Town

Jasper

The fireworks have just started. Big, slow blooms of light against the deep black sky, the kind of night where your breath hangs in the air and the smell of smoke clings to everything.

Lucy's perched on my hip, her arms around my neck and one of her boots thudding rhythmically against my thigh. She's still got her gloves on, miraculously, and is clutching a sparkler that fizzled out two minutes ago but she refuses to let go of.

Beside me, Theo's got Ivy tucked into his side. Geoff's nudging Christa again, winding her up— she's quieter than usual tonight, but Geoff's been on a mission to crack her since we arrived.

"I'm just saying," he murmurs theatrically, "Bonfire Night moping is punishable by public shaming and enforced marshmallow consumption."

"I'm not moping," Christa replies, clearly moping.

"Then why do you look like a Jane Austen heroine left out in the frost?"

Despite herself, she laughs. One-nil to my brother.

Ivy throws Geoff a look. "You're ridiculous."

"Charming," he corrects.

Theo snorts. "More like persistent."

Another firework goes up—golden this time, fizzing and falling like a shower of sparks. Lucy gasps dramatically, holding tighter around my neck.

"They're so loud!" she shouts in my ear.

"They're meant to be," I say, adjusting my hold on her. "That's the whole point."

From the loudspeakers near the clubhouse, the village volunteer starts reading the classic lines, voice warbling slightly over the mic:

"Remember, remember, the fifth of November, Gunpowder, treason and plot..."

Lucy immediately jumps in, shouting along:

"*Rememba*, *rememba*, the fifth of *Novemba*, Gunpowder, *teasin'*, and plot!"

I glance up at her. "*Treason*, Lu."

She frowns. "That's what I said."

Theo turns to grin at us. "Honestly, I like her version better."

Geoff nods. "Less political."

Another firework bursts—silver this time, cracking loud across the sky.

Lucy squeals, delighted, kicking her boots and bouncing slightly in my arms.

"Alright, Ladybug," I say, shifting her weight. "Shall we get that toffee apple before the mob hits the food stalls?"

"Yes please!"

I start weaving us through the edge of the crowd, careful not to elbow anyone still enjoying the last of the fireworks. The smell of fried onions and smoke thickens as we near the stalls, that unmistakable Bonfire Night blend of charred meat, sugar, and cider.

Lucy leans in, breath hot against my cheek. "Do you want me to tell you the story of Guy Fox?"

"Guy Fawkes. Absolutely."

She nods like she's just agreed to deliver a TED Talk.

"So. Once upon a time," she begins, "there was a man called Guy Fox. He didn't like the king. So he and some other naughty men got some... gunpowdies—"

"Gunpowder," I say gently.

"Gunpowder, yes. And they hid it in a basement under the Houses of Palmen."

"Parliament," I correct.

"That's what I said."

"Of course."

"And he was gonna blow it up," she continues, widening her eyes for dramatic effect. "But someone *snitched*. So, the king's guards found the gunpowder, and they said, 'Oi! What are you doing, Guy Fox?' And then he got arrested and they were *not* happy."

"I imagine not."

"And that's why we have fireworks. Because he was naughty and got caught."

"That's one way of putting it," I say.

She beams at me, utterly satisfied with her version of events.

We reach the front of the food truck queue just as the crowds start surging over. I buy her a toffee apple, the woman behind the counter winking at Lucy as she hands it over like it's made of gold.

Lucy frees herself from her gloves which she shoves into my free hand and then clutches the sticky apple with both hands like a holy relic, eyes shining.

"I'm not sharing," she declares sternly.

"Didn't ask."

She grins, mouth already full of sugar.

We make our way back toward the others. Lucy's fingers are a sticky mess now. There is probably a healthy amount on my jacket as well. But I wouldn't want it any other way.

As we're heading across the edge of the green, a group comes into view, moving in the opposite direction—Coop, Omar,

Ben, and a few women I don't recognise, chatting over each other and still glowing from the fireworks.

"Jasper!" Coop calls out, lifting an arm and waving.

I lift a hand in return, giving him a nod.

Lucy perks up. "Who's that?"

"Coop," I say. "Plays on the team with me."

"And the other people?"

"The one in the hat is Omar. That's Ben next to him."

She squints. "Are they your friends?"

"Sort of. Mates from the football club."

Her brow furrows, very serious. "Is that lady his wife?" She's pointing with the apple now—vaguely in the direction of Amelia, who's got her arm looped through Ben's.

"His girlfriend," I say. "Her name's Amelia."

"She looks nice."

"She is."

"And the lady in the big scarf?"

"No idea."

She makes a thoughtful hum, rests her chin on my shoulder again, and crunches into her apple like she's gathering intel for some future mission.

By the time we make it back to the others, the last of the fireworks have burned themselves out and the green's thinning fast. Theo looks up as we approach and holds out his hands.

"Ladybug," he says, soft but firm. "Time to go home."

Lucy lets out a theatrical sigh, then leans in for one last squeeze around my neck. She smells like toffee apple and bonfire smoke. It's gross and perfect.

"Can I come again next year?" she whispers.

"Every year," I murmur back.

She lets go reluctantly and I hand her over to Theo, who takes her with the ease of a father who, until recently, was single and the sole parent to this adorably little girl. That was until he met Ivy and now they are a family. Not yet in an official form, but Geoff and I are sure that it won't be long.

Ivy pulls Lucy's hood up and wipes some apple off her cheek with a napkin pulled from nowhere. Lu giggles and keeps on nibbling her toffee covered fruit whilst Ivy cleans her up.

We head toward the car park together. Geoff's offered Christa a lift, and she's clearly grateful not to have to navigate the train home on her own. Theo, Ivy and Lu are in the second car. They are already debating which chip shop is open on the way.

At the row of parked cars, we pause in that awkward pre-departure circle.

Geoff slaps a hand on my shoulder. "You need to come to the café next week. Theo's got that bloody ridiculous hazelnut thing back on the menu. You can come sulk in a corner and complain it's too sweet."

"I don't sulk," I say mildly.

"You *brood*, then."

Theo gives me a one-armed hug, Lucy already strapped into the backseat, chatting to herself.

"Come by soon," he says. "We'll do dinner."

"I might hold you to that."

"You always say that," Ivy teases.

I shrug. "Still true."

Geoff leans on the car door. "Honestly, it's embarrassing that you live out here in the wild and haven't even got a bloody sourdough starter. Civilisation misses you."

"You live in a two-bed in Highbury," I point out.

"And it's full of soul."

"Full of damp," Theo mutters, climbing into the driver's seat.

They all laugh, and just like that, they're off—headlights sweeping past me as they pull out, red taillights vanishing down the road.

I shove my hands in my pockets and breathe out into the dark.

It's quiet now. The kind of quiet you don't get in London. No taxis, no shouting, no sirens humming under your skin. Just the creak of branches in the wind and the occasional scuffle of something in the hedgerow. Rabbit. Fox. Possibly something hellbent on getting into my bins again.

The walk home isn't long—ten minutes at most, along the edge of the lane, past the stone wall I still haven't got around to repairing, then up the gravel drive.

I miss them, sometimes. The noise of it all. Theo talking too much, Geoff being smug in three languages, Lucy leaving her socks in places physics can't explain. But I don't miss London.

Moving out here was the best decision I've ever made. No neighbours on the other side of a paper-thin wall. No impossible parking. No fighting ten people for a seat on the tube. Just space. Time. A house so big it still feels a bit like trespassing.

The porch light flicks on as I step up to the door. It's on a motion-sensor, but it still startles me every time.

I'm pulling off one glove when my phone buzzes in my pocket.

I answer on the second ring. "Hey Ben"

"Jasper, mate. You free for a favour?"

I pause, pushing the door open with my shoulder, the warmth of the house spilling over me like a wave.

"That depends," I say, toeing off my boots. "Is it the kind of favour that involves bailing someone out?"

Ben laughs. "No, no. Nothing that dramatic. Just... the annexe."

I pause in the hallway, halfway out of my coat.

"Right," I say slowly. "What about it?"

Ben exhales down the line, like he's been half-running or trying not to talk too loudly near someone.

"So, Amelia's friend Miranda... she's just come out of a divorce. Proper shitshow. Husband's a complete arsehole. She's got an eight-year-old son and needs somewhere to stay. Somewhere steady. Quiet. Safe."

I lean against the hallway wall, still holding my gloves.

Ben goes on, "We were all at the bonfire earlier, and it just sort of… came up. Omar mentioned the flat. Amelia would feel better knowing Miranda is close by so we thought we'd ask."

I say nothing, so Ben adds, "Look, I know you were not planning to rent it out. And of course you can say no. But… she's good people. Bit shell-shocked. And she doesn't want charity, just a chance to land on her feet."

I stare down the hallway into the dark. The annexe's technically attached, practically its own little world.

After a beat, I ask, "Her child is quiet?"

Ben huffs a laugh. "Yes, and it is shared custody, so he won't be there all the time."

I rub a hand over the back of my neck. "How soon are we talking?"

"Soonish."

I sigh. "Tell her to come have a look."

Ben's smile is audible. "Knew you'd say yes."

"I didn't say yes."

"You didn't say no."

I sigh. "Tell her to come by. Look at the place. No promises."

"I'll let her know."

"Fine."

"Thanks, mate. Seriously. You're doing something good."

I snort. "Careful. If you start getting sentimental, I'll invoice you for emotional support."

Ben laughs. "That's fair."

"Night, Ben."

"Night, Jasper."

I hang up and slide the phone into my back pocket.

I rub a hand over my face, already regretting offering to let this woman even have a look.

I lock the door, flick off the hall light, when my phone rings again.

"Callum!" I greet my best friend.

"I need your help, mate," he replies instead of a greeting.

"Well, you are in luck, apparently I agree to anything today."

4

Merry Ex-Mas, You Filthy Animal

Miranda

SJ is sitting cross-legged in the middle of the bedroom floor, surrounded by what appears to be the entire contents of his toy chest, three drawers, and the deep void under his bed. There's a dinosaur in each hand, a book open on his lap, and a half-eaten banana on the duvet behind him, because obviously this is now a buffet.

He looks up. "I don't know what to bring, Mum. What if I forget something important?"

"You won't. We'll make a list. Lists solve everything."

He squints at me. "Even climate change?"

"Almost everything," I amend, gently tugging a sock off the corner of his pillow. "Start with the things you use all the time. What couldn't you live without?"

He considers this like a small, serious accountant preparing for an audit. "Blue Rexy. My Spider-Man mug. And the soft pillow, not the lumpy one."

I nod, dutifully setting Blue Rexy in the 'must-pack' pile. "Excellent choices. Mug we'll wrap in your jumper."

He frowns at the rest of the room. "What about the pirate ship? It's too big."

"You'll still come here, love. Dad's keeping your room."

"Yeah but... what if it feels different?"

It already does feel different.

Since I caught Sim-Sim with his trousers around his ankles we have been cohabitating. The atmosphere had been tense, even if we tried to not have any arguments in front of SJ. But still. It hasn't been the same.

I sit next to SJ on the floor, knees cracking like bubble wrap. "It will feel different. But different doesn't have to mean worse."

He doesn't reply. Just strokes the edge of his book absent-mindedly.

I don't know how to make this part easier. For him or for me. I don't want to overpromise, or underplay it, or tell him it'll all be fine when I don't know what Tuesday looks like.

But I know this: I won't let this break him. Break us.

"Dad's still your dad," I say gently. "And I'm still your mum. And wherever you are, we'll make it feel like home. Deal?"

He nods. Still quiet. But he leans into me, head on my shoulder. Just for a second.

I breathe in the smell of banana, crayons, and the weird plasticky tang of that slime he's obsessed with.

"Alright," I say, patting his knee. "Let's get strategic. We've got one box, one bag, and one slightly overstuffed tote bag. Choose wisely."

He grins, and just like that, we're moving again.

We pack in a rhythm. I fold clothes while he lines up action figures like they're about to enter a very inefficient Noah's Ark. He chooses his favourite books. I sneak in an extra pair of pyjamas because I know how this goes.

We argue about whether the giant stuffed sloth will fit—it will not. He insists on bringing a framed photo of the three of us from a holiday in Wales. Sim-Sim, still pretending, SJ grinning with ice cream all over his face, me looking... hopeful. I hesitate for half a breath, then nod.

"Let's wrap it in bubble wrap. We'll stick it on your shelf at the new place."

"What's it like?" he asks, not looking at me.

"It's smaller," I say, wrapping the photo in an old scarf and laying it gently in the box. "And a bit less... *fancy*. No marble countertops or taps that cost more than a family car. But it's in a proper village. You know Little Hadlow from when we visited Amelia. It's a cute village. One with an actual butcher, and a post office that sells weird sweets from the eighties."

He looks vaguely interested but doesn't bite.

"There's loads of green space," I add, nudging a pair of pyjamas into the corner. "You can run around without someone reporting us to the building management. Amelia and Ben live five minutes away. And you'll get to play with Smutty."

That gets a reaction. He grins. "He's so grumpy."

"Exactly. Like a tiny, disapproving feline overlord. He'll love you. Eventually. Probably. If you bring snacks."

SJ pulls at a loose thread on his jumper, still frowning a bit. "All my friends are here."

I sit back on my heels and nod. "I know. And you'll still see them. You're still going to the same school, remember?"

"But—"

"Even if it means your dad has to hire a driver," I say, trying not to sound smug about it. "Which he has. Full suit, little hat. You'll be the most chauffeured eight-year-old this side of the royal family."

He snorts. "That's weird."

"It's posh. And it means you're not stuck on a train. You'll see your dad on weekends and you'll spend a week a month at your dad's as well."

He thinks about that, chewing the inside of his cheek. "Do I get a key to the new place?"

"Of course you do."

"Can I make a den?"

"Only if I'm allowed in."

"You're not," he says, deadpan.

I press a hand to my heart. "Betrayed. Day one."

He grins, but it's lopsided, like he's still trying to piece all this together.

I know the feeling.

We sit in the half-packed room for a moment, surrounded by soft toys and a future we're still packing up. The light's gone flat outside, grey and dull. One of his T-shirts drapes off the side of the bed like it's thinking about jumping.

I reach over and brush a bit of fluff from his hair. "It'll be alright, you know."

He shrugs. "I know. Just... weird."

"Yeah," I say softly. "Weird's about right."

There's a knock on the doorframe.

Sim-Sim has got that careful look on, the one he wears in meetings when he's trying not to spook a client.

"Miranda," he says, voice low. "Can I talk to you for a minute?"

I nod. I am done talking really, but we need to find a way to be civil to each other, even if it is just for SJ. So I follow Sim-Sim to the kitchen.

He doesn't rush. Just stands near the table, hands in his pockets like they might stop him saying something stupid. For a second, it's so quiet I can hear SJ humming faintly from the bedroom.

"I just..." He takes a breath. "Are you really sure?"

I don't answer immediately.

He looks tired. Not the performative kind, not a subtle "feel sorry for me" tactic. Just... worn. Like the last few weeks have chipped at him in ways he didn't see coming.

"As sure as I was when I signed the divorce papers," I say eventually.

He nods, once. Looks down.

"I swear to you, it was a one-off. That girl—it wasn't anything. It wasn't even *someone*, not really. Just a mistake."

I stay still.

"I never cheated before," he goes on. "Not once. I know I messed up, but... it's not who I am. I was stupid. And I was tired. And you were gone. And I know none of that makes it better, but I still... I love you."

The words land heavily. Not sharp. Not dramatic. Just plain. Like he really believes they still mean something.

I glance away, just for a second.

The weight of it hits all at once... the years, the history, the life we built. The dinners, the birthdays, the endless shared decisions that shaped everything.

I don't reply because I don't know what to say.

He takes a step closer. Careful. Like I'm a wounded animal and he's hoping not to get bitten.

"You don't have to go," he says. "Not yet. You could stay. Just for a bit. In the guest room, like before. And we could... feel our way back. Slowly. No pressure. Just space. Time."

I close my eyes.

There's a version of me that wants to say yes. The part that still remembers the good days. The part that wants to keep SJ's world whole. The part that's tired of being strong all the bloody time.

But I also remember standing in that bedroom and the sound he made when he called her *baby girl.*

When I open my eyes, he's watching me like he's holding his breath.

"I can't," I say softly. "I can't try to find my way back to something I haven't forgiven."

He flinches, barely. But I see it.

"I don't know... I might eventually forgive you," I add. "But I haven't yet. And I won't pretend I have just to make it easier."

He nods. Slowly.

"Alright," he says. "I just—I had to try."

I look at him for a long moment. "I know."

We stand in silence for a beat too long.

Then I turn to go.

Because I'm still not entirely sure what comes next.

But I know it isn't this.

5

Have Yourself a Merry Little Flat Let

Miranda

The car door creaks like it's in physical pain as I push it open.

"Alright, Geraldine," I mutter under my breath, giving the dashboard an encouraging pat. "You've done your best. You may rest." London to Little Hadlow in a car I bought for the price of a fancy hairdryer. She rattles, wheezes, and the windscreen wipers have one speed: dramatic panic. But she got us here. Just about.

SJ's already halfway out, unbuckling himself with purpose. His earlier sadness seems to have been replaced by genuine curiosity. Let's just hope it stays this way.

I sit for a moment, taking in the house.

It's... well, it's stunning. Sort of a fancy modern villa disguised as a countryside retreat—white render, huge windows, sleek lines softened by ivy and those tasteful potted olive trees you only ever see in magazines. There's a gravel drive, and the kind of elegant symmetry that says *I don't own IKEA furniture.*

SJ leans forward, pressing his face to the glass. "It's huge."

"That's because it's not all ours," I say, already texting the girls.

Me

We've arrived! Beat the movers. Come and welcome me to country life. I need the moral support

The annexe is on the right side of the main house, but with its own sleek black door and a little path lined with lavender. It looks... solid.

I hesitate, thumb hovering over the bell.

I haven't met Jasper, our new landlord. When I came to see the place, he was apparently off on some business trip in Asia, which sounded either very jet-set or very evasive. His best mate's girlfriend Stella showed me round and did the whole agreement.

He's a mystery. And although Ben and Omar assured me that he is a trustworthy guy, I'd rather prefer I could judge for myself.

I take a deep breath and press the bell.

SJ stands beside me, backpack on both shoulders, giving the door a squinty once-over like it might be booby-trapped.

"Do you think he's nice?" he whispers.

"Ben likes him." That seems to be enough for SJ. He hero-worships Ben and Coop.

Footsteps.

A pause.

The door opens.

It's not Jasper.

"Hello!" beams Stella. "Lovely to see you again!"

I blink, regrouping. "Stella—hi. You too."

She turns her bright smile on SJ.

"And you must be SJ. I've heard a lot about you."

SJ perks up immediately. "From Mum?"

"Of course," she says. "She told me you're a Mario Kart champion and take your dinosaur collection *very* seriously."

He gives me a satisfied look, like he's just been correctly identified as royalty.

Stella steps aside and gestures us in. "Come on in. Everything's ready for you."

I hesitate. "Is Jasper not back yet?"

"No—still in Singapore. Something about a supplier meeting running over. He is now coming on a later flight but he asked me to pass on his welcome and to say that he's very sorry not to be here."

Of course he is. I nod, keeping my expression polite.

She leads us into the open plan kitchen/living space. Sleek, neutral, much nicer than anything labelled "annexe" usually deserves to be.

"We made a few upgrades," Stella says, ushering us into the kitchen area. "Bigger fridge. Jasper thought you might need extra freezer space for fish fingers and emergency ice cream."

I glance around. "Very astute of him."

"New dishwasher too. The last one sounded like it was processing its feelings."

SJ trails behind us, quietly impressed. I can see him clocking the cupboards, the shiny tap, the way the floor doesn't creak. He disappears down the hall.

"All the rooms were repainted," she adds. "We went neutral. Think calming, with aspirations of taste."

I raise a brow. "Very Instagram divorce-core."

She grins. "Exactly."

SJ calls from the main bedroom. "I want this one! It's got a bathroom!"

I join him in the master bedroom where he's standing dead centre like he's about to plant a flag.

"That's *my* room," I say.

"But it's got the toilet!"

"And I'm the one who'll actually clean it. Out you go."

He groans theatrically but trudges back into the hallway, dragging his feet like I've just evicted him from a castle. I guide him into the other room.

"This one's yours." I usher him into the second bedroom.

He eyes it like he's assessing the structural integrity. "It's alright."

"You'll make it brilliant," I say. "Soon as we get your dinosaurs in formation."

He drops his bag with a thud and gives a resigned nod, clearly filing this injustice away for future therapy.

Then the doorbell rings.

I know it's probably the movers. Or the girls. But still—I hesitate.

It doesn't quite feel like my flat yet. I haven't earned the muscle memory of it. The familiarity. The right to swing the door open like I belong here.

I glance at Stella.

She gives me an encouraging smile. "It's all yours now."

So I square my shoulders, walk to the door, and open it.

Omar is front and centre, one arm balancing a giant shopping bag, the other clutching a toolbox that has seen better days. Before I can say anything, he leans in and gives me a kiss on the cheek.

"Alright, Miranda," he says warmly. "Point me to wherever things need assembling, and I shall build you a new life, one Allen key at a time."

"My flatpack hero," I say, genuinely tempted to cry on him but holding it together.

Bri appears just behind him, carrying something awkward and lumpy under a blanket, looking far too pleased with herself.

She greets me with a one-armed hug and a waft of expensive perfume and sarcasm.

"Hello, darling," she says. "Nice door. Solid hinges. Very 'divorced but dignified'."

I narrow my eyes at the blanket. "What is that?"

"Nothing."

"Bri—"

Before she can dig herself any deeper into whatever nonsense she's hiding under that blanket, Stella and SJ appear behind us, joining the fray in the open-plan living space that currently contains nothing but an echo, some keys, and Omar's very organised chaos.

I gesture between them. "Right, quick intros. Stella, this is Bri and Omar. Bri and Omar, this is Stella—she's been my saviour on all things logistical and was the one who showed me round."

Omar straightens slightly, giving Stella a warm smile. "Oh. You're Callum's partner, aren't you?"

"Partner, secretary, occasional conscience," she replies, breezy. "He couldn't run his life without me."

"Sounds familiar," Bri laughs before poking Omar in his side.

He pulls her in his arms before returning his attention to Stella. "Nice to meet you."

"Pleasure," she replies.

And then Bri clears her throat loudly—the sort of theatrical preamble that usually ends in something wildly unnecessary.

"Right," she says, shifting her grip on the mystery bundle. "Now that we're all here, I'd like to present a little something."

Omar smirks knowing.

"A housewarming gift," she goes on, undeterred. "For Miranda and SJ."

SJ perks up immediately. "Is it biscuits?"

"No," Bri says, beaming. "Better."

SJ's eyes go wide. "Is it a Nintendo?"

"Different kind of responsibility," she says.

Then, with a grand flourish, she whips the blanket off—revealing a cat carrier. Inside, two wide-eyed kittens blink up at us, pressed together in a huddle of tiny paws and confusion.

One's a smoky grey tabby, the other a ridiculous marmalade ginger with too-big ears and the expression of someone startled by fireworks.

SJ gasps so loudly it's almost a squeak. "KITTENS?!"

I stare. "Bri."

She shrugs, entirely unapologetic. "You *said* you might take two."

"MIGHT!" I repeat. "As in, a theoretical discussion over wine. Not a binding kitten acquisition contract. I haven't even asked the landlord yet." When Bri told us that Zucca couldn't keep it in his metaphorical pants and managed to get Bella knocked up before Bri could get them both spayed, we all felt sorry for her. But I never really entertained the idea of adding two kittens to my chaos.

Behind me, Stella laughs. It's a low, knowing sort of laugh with a glint in her eye that says *Oh, you sweet summer tenant.*

"It'll be fine," she replies breezily.

I squint at her. “Shouldn’t I check with Jasper?”

She waves a hand like I’ve just suggested I get permission to own a kettle. “Honestly, if he were that concerned, he should’ve made the effort to be here.”

Omar coughs into his coffee. “Are you saying you’re staging a kitten coup?”

“It’s not a coup,” Bri says primly. “It’s a gentle, purring act of kindness.”

“Tell that to the furniture,” I mutter, peering back into the carrier where the ginger one is now gnawing enthusiastically on the bars like it’s in training for a prison break.

SJ crouches beside it, eyes wide. “What are their names?”

Bri crouches too, peering in with the air of a benevolent animal smuggler. “The tabby’s a boy. The ginger’s a girl. I figured you and your mum should each name one.”

SJ turns to me, solemn. “Can I pick the boy?”

“Sure.” There is no way I can now say he can’t have these kittens and Bri very much knew this. She bloody owes me big time!

SJ beams when Bri opens the carrier carefully and lifts out the grey tabby—who immediately starts squirming like a furry eel—and gently hands him over. SJ cradles the kitten awkwardly but reverently, like it’s both sacred and possibly explosive.

“I’m naming him Thor,” he announces.

“Big name for a small cat,” Omar murmurs.

“He’ll grow into it,” SJ says, deadly serious. “He’s already mighty.”

Thor chirps and then tries to climb up SJ's hoodie using only claws and ambition.

"And what about her?" Bri asks, lifting the ginger kitten from the carrier and handing her to me.

She's so light it's almost shocking—all fluff and curiosity, her whiskers twitching as she blinks up at me. Each of her paws ends in neat white spots, like she's wearing tiny socks. Ridiculously pink toe beans peek out as she stretches against my hand.

I sigh, already gone.

"Twinklesocks," I say.

Omar blinks. "I'm sorry, what?"

"Twinklesocks," I repeat, deadpan. "Don't question it. It came to me."

Bri looks like Christmas just came early. "I *love* it."

Thor chirps again and headbutts SJ's chin. Twinklesocks yawns in my arms like she's politely pretending she didn't just try to bite my thumb.

Bri folds her arms, looking smugger than someone who's just won a national award for emotional manipulation. "Welcome to the cat lady club."

I narrow my eyes. "What did you do with the other three?"

She doesn't even flinch. "Fi took one. Lizzie and Coop adopted the other two—technically Lizzie did, but Coop's already started referring to himself as a 'cat dad' unironically."

Omar groans into his coffee. "This is an infestation disguised as a lifestyle."

Bri beams. "We are now officially five cat ladies. Resistance is futile."

"Five!" I echo. "Is this a friend group or an organised cult?"

"Why not both?" she says brightly. "We've got matching lint rollers and everything."

Thor attempts to climb SJ's hoodie again, back legs flailing as he clings to the zip like he's scaling Everest.

Bri claps her hands. "And! As another housewarming gift, I brought supplies."

Omar sighs, already turning for the door. "I'll get them."

"Love you," Bri calls after him.

I eye her warily. "What kind of supplies?"

"Kitten stuff," she says cheerfully. "Litter trays, food, toys, the works. You think I'd turn up with live animals and no infrastructure? Please."

I blink. "That... actually feels responsible."

"Don't sound so shocked. I've grown."

Omar reappears a moment later, arms full: three litter trays stacked inside each other like some sort of plastic nesting doll, a massive bag of litter, tins of food, and a small bin full of crinkly, jingly, probably-already-annoying toys.

I stare. "Three trays?"

Bri nods. "Cats are territorial. You need one per cat *plus one* to avoid civil unrest."

SJ looks impressed. "That's cool."

"It's cat maths," Bri says, handing him a packet of tiny feathered mice. "Very serious."

Stella, still lingering with mild amusement, glances down the hall. "There's a utility room with the washing machine. Might be good to put two in there?"

"Brilliant," Bri says. "And maybe one in the family bathroom, for... overflow?"

"Perfect," Stella replies, with the ease of someone who has never, and will never, clean a litter tray.

"Come on, SJ," Bri says, grabbing a tray. "Let's set up the royal thrones."

He turns to me, glowing with purpose. "Can you hold Thor?"

"Sure," I say, taking the wiggly kitten out of SJ's arms. "But don't get used to this much excitement about cat toilets. The novelty wears off."

"I'll always help," SJ promises, bouncing off after Bri, arms full of feline sanitation gear.

"He'll forget he said that within three days," I mutter, adjusting my grip on Thor, who is now gnawing enthusiastically on a strand of my hair.

Stella laughs. "Of course he will. That's the parenting deal."

"And who ends up scooping the clumps?" I ask the room, to no one in particular.

Twinklesocks meows sleepily from her spot against my chest and flicks her tail like she knows exactly who.

6

The Twelve Days of Jet Lag

Jasper

The driver's playing something soothing—piano, strings, the sort of instrumental soundtrack that thinks it's helping. It isn't. My head's buzzing, my eyes feel like sandpaper, and every muscle in my back is staging a slow, organised rebellion.

I shift in my seat, trying to find a position that doesn't feel medically concerning. First class or not, two weeks of hotels, back-to-back meetings and the jet lag equivalent of being repeatedly slapped with a wet pillow has finally caught up with me.

I don't sleep well on planes. Never have. Something about the hum, the recycled air, the relentless sense of being trapped in a tube—it all keeps my brain twitching just enough to stop rest from happening. I drift. Hover. Float in that half-sleep where your neck clicks at the wrong angle and you have strange dreams about spreadsheets that can talk.

Callum, of course, slept the whole flight. Curled up with his noise-cancelling headphones and a blanket he insisted was "NASA-approved." He offered me one of those inflatable neck pillows as if that would fix decades of deeply entrenched restlessness and control issues. I think I just stared at him until he put it away.

The truth is, I didn't really need to be in Singapore.

The deal wasn't mine. It's Callum's company, his client, his success, and he's more than capable of handling it. Has been for years. But we've always had that arrangement when one of us needs an extra set of eyes, a bit of backup, the other shows up. It's not about necessity. It's about momentum. And power.

Sometimes, just having a second person in the room tips things. Not because I said anything particularly clever—though I like to think I was at least moderately intimidating—but because the client clocked that Callum had support, that he wasn't flinging proposals across the table solo.

Strength in numbers. Posturing, basically. But the good kind. The kind that lands you an extra zero at the end of a contract.

And it worked. The client signed. Callum looked five years younger and three inches taller. And all I really did was throw some disapproving looks across the table.

He still sees me as some sort of mentor, which is both flattering and vaguely hilarious. He doesn't need me. But I suppose it's easy to forget your own competence when the stakes get high.

So I turned up. I smiled in the right places. I drank very average coffee from very expensive boardrooms. And now I'm crawling back along the M25 in a car that smells faintly of fabric softener and end-of-trip fatigue.

The driver clears his throat. "Traffic's moving. Should have you back in just under an hour."

I grunt something that might pass for gratitude and close my eyes again, though sleep is still off somewhere over the Channel.

It's just before midnight when we finally roll up the drive. I step out into the cool night air, stretch slightly, and blink up at the stars like I might find a second wind somewhere between Orion and Heathrow.

And then I notice it.

The lights.

On, steady, glowing out from the small flat on the right—the annexe, as my solicitor insists on calling it, though Stella's tried more than once to pitch it as a "self-contained executive let." It's not. It's a decent two-bedroom with its own entrance and slightly too much beige.

For half a second, I frown, confused. Then I remember.

Right. The tenant.

Stella sorted it all while I was away. Said it was an easy one. She assured me Miranda is lovely and won't be any trouble. She told me that part at least five times, which does make me suspicious.

So I'd asked Callum if he thought Stella was pulling something. Wouldn't be the first time. She once tried to set me up with one of her relatives under the guise of "urgent marketing consultancy." That woman had a Pomeranian in a pram and believed Gwyneth Paltrow had been misunderstood.

Callum had rolled his eyes at my question. "Mate, she's not matchmaking."

I want to believe him. Maybe my brothers are right. I am turning into a bit of a hermit.

After I say goodbye to the driver, I wheel my suitcase to the door and let myself in. The house is still and cold, just as I left it. No sounds of life from next door, but then it's nearly midnight; I'm hardly expecting her to be hosting a party already.

I drop my keys onto the side table and head upstairs, too tired to do anything but autopilot. Stripping off the last of the travel-wrinkled layers, I step into the shower and let the water run hot enough to sting.

It doesn't fix the jet lag or the deep ache behind my eyes, but it's something.

When I finally crawl into bed, everything hurts in the way that suggests I'm either getting old or allergic to air travel. Possibly both.

Still, I make a note to myself: tomorrow, I'll do the civilised thing. At the very least, I should introduce myself.

That's what normal people do, isn't it?

The treadmill hums beneath me, steady and joyless. My feet slap out a rhythm, sharp against the rubber. It's just gone six, but the world outside is still thick with night; black sky pressing in against the gym's long windows.

The air in here is cooler than I like. I didn't bother waiting for the heating to kick in. Just yanked on my kit and started moving. Better to sweat into the cold than sit still and listen to the silence claw at the walls.

Normally, I'd swim. Nothing clears the mind like cutting through water—smooth, silent, solitary. But the local pool doesn't open until seven, and I can't be arsed to sit around waiting for chlorinated serenity.

I'd have had one built by now. A proper pool house out in the garden, something sleek and warm and mine, but the parish council got twitchy. "Out of character with the village aesthetic," they said. "Obtrusive." As if I'd planned to install a disco and a hot dog van alongside it.

So. No pool. Just this. A tiny home gym.

I increase the speed slightly, the incline a little more. Make it bite.

A dull ache starts in my right calf. The good kind. Reminds me I'm not entirely ornamental. That something still works.

I used to know what my days were for.

There were meetings, pitches, problems with edges. Things that needed solving, urgently, with consequences if I didn't. People who looked to me like I was the adult in the room. And I suppose I was.

Now?

Now there's this: silence, sweat, motion without direction. A treadmill in every sense.

I don't need to work. That's the headline, isn't it? Clever man makes clever thing, retires before forty, becomes a cautionary tale for ambitious twenty-somethings who think they'd enjoy having nothing to do.

No one says what comes after.

The money's fine. The freedom's fine. The doing nothing is... not.

I've invested. Dabbled. Stuck my name on a few things to make other people feel better about theirs. But nothing's lit that part of my brain that used to wake me up at three in the morning because it couldn't wait to try something.

Now I wake up because I can't remember why I sleep.

I increase the pace again. Not by much. Just enough to feel it in my chest.

After another twenty minutes of running that gets all my muscles burning. I finally push the button and the machine slows down. I need a shower; but first a coffee.

As I head downstairs in my running shorts, I toe off my running shoes, pull the soaking wet T-shirt over my head and drop it in the basket in the utility room.

My skin is cooling in patches where the sweat's started to dry. The kitchen tiles are cold underfoot, a sharp little reminders that November doesn't care if you've just burned five hundred calories trying to outrun a vague sense of purposelessness.

I flip on the lights and basically can taste the coffee on my tongue already. Still overheated, I open the door to the garden. A gust of cold air rushes in, biting against my skin. I exhale sharply. Better.

I pop the lid on the coffee pod jar, pick one at random and slide it into the machine. Familiar movement. Something automatic. Hands doing what they've done a thousand mornings before.

And then—

Something soft brushes against my ankle.

I freeze. Not metaphorically. No, I'm at a full stop. Like a statue.

My first thought—entirely rational, given the hour and my blood sugar levels—is rat. Some bold little menace from the neighbour's compost heap staging a kitchen coup.

I glance down, preparing to launch a mug if necessary.

It's not a rat.

It is... orange.

No. *Ginger.*

Fluffy. Round. With white paws like it's wearing the latest feline shoe line. And currently staring up at me like *I'm* the surprise.

We lock eyes.

It meows.

High-pitched. Piercing. The sound of entitlement in fur form.

I take a slow step back, as if disengaging from a wild animal on a nature programme. It follows. Purring.

"You... don't live with me," I inform it, very reasonably.

It blinks up at me with the blank confidence of something that's never paid rent in its life... then leans forward and licks my shin.

I recoil instinctively. "Oh God. No. That's—*don't* do that."

It does it again. Enthusiastically.

Apparently, post-run leg sweat is the breakfast of champions.

"Brilliant," I mutter, swiping gently at it with a tea towel as if I'm warding off a particularly persistent foot fetishist. "Absolutely not how I imagined starting my morning."

The kitten attacks the tea towel with alarming enthusiasm, latching onto it like it's just declared a blood feud.

"Oh, for—" I lift the towel, kitten still attached, a dangling, soft orange bauble of wrath.

It growls. Actually growls. A noise that might be threatening if it weren't coming from something that weighs less than a decent sandwich.

"Right. That's enough," I mutter, peeling tiny claws off cotton. It flails mid-air and, against my better judgement and every principle I hold about not hugging wild animals, I draw it in and hold it against my chest.

It goes limp instantly. Snuggles in.

Purrs.

Loudly. Deeply. I stare down at it, baffled.

"You manipulative little furball," I whisper.

The purring intensifies.

Of course it does.

Then, from somewhere beyond the open door, a whisper-shout cuts through the silence:

"Twinklesocks! Pss-pss-pss—Twinklesocks!"

It comes again, louder, still in that frantic stage whisper people use when trying not to wake small children or enrage large neighbours.

"*Twinklesocks!*"

There's a rustle. Movement. A crouched figure emerging from the hedgerow like a burglar with a moral conscience.

I walk to the door, kitten still anchored to my chest, and lean out.

"Is this what you're looking for?" I chuckle.

The figure startles upright with a small gasp. Straightens too fast and wobbles slightly, caught in the act.

That's when I see her properly for the first time.

Hair in a chaotic bun, tendrils escaping in every direction. Big eyes. Shocked expression. And the faint, universal look of someone who *definitely* didn't plan to meet anyone before 7 a.m.

She blinks. "Hi."

Then she points weakly at the orange fluff glued to my chest. "That's... yes. Twinklesocks."

I glance down at the kitten

She looks up at me. Slow blink. Like she's confirming it, "Yes, that's my ridiculous name."

My gaze drifts back to the woman: breathless, hair in full mutiny, weird pyjamas, slippers, eyes far too wide for this hour. And still, she is adorable... no, stunning.

Brilliant.

The kitten's trouble.

But the woman?

Quite possibly worse.

7

Do You Hear What I Hear? (It's a Landlord)

Miranda

I freeze.

Absolutely, completely, brain-has-left-the-building freeze.

Standing in front of me—barefoot, shirtless, a ginger kitten draped across his chest as if he's auditioning for a calendar titled *Paws and Abs*—is a man who can only be described as... illegal.

Dark hair with golden streaks like he's spent the summer surfing instead of paying council tax. A jawline with actual stubble, not the sort of half-hearted fluff most men call "‘beard goals". And eyes… deep brown, bordering on black. Eyes that make you forget your name, postcode, and possibly your own child's birthday.

This is Jasper?

This is my landlord?

I take a step forward to collect Twinklesocks. That's all I mean to do. A simple handoff.

But instead of reaching for her, my traitorous hand taps his chest muscle.

Taps.

His *pec*.

Like I'm checking the ripeness of a melon.

I freeze again. The kitten blinks. He blinks. I want the ground to swallow me whole.

"Oh my God," I mutter, pulling my hand back like it's been burned. "Sorry. That wasn't—I didn't mean to—sorry."

And just as I think it can't get worse, I remember what I'm wearing.

Reindeer pyjamas. Bloody reindeer pyjamas.

Under an open winter coat that makes me look like I've escaped from an off-brand Nordic crime drama. My slippers—the ones Amelia calls "old man chic" with deep concern—are soggy from the grass and currently squelching every time I shift my weight.

I look like a madwoman.

Because I *am* one. One who sprinted into the garden at half six in the morning because her eight-year-old ran from the hallway in a whisper-panic to report that Twinklesocks had jumped out the open bathroom window "and might be gone forever."

I didn't ask why the bathroom window was open. I didn't stop to grab a hairbrush or dignity. I just bolted.

And now I'm standing here, dressed like Christmas had a breakdown, having just pawed the chest of a man who looks like he belongs on a yacht. In Monaco.

Fantastic.

He shifts his weight slightly, still holding Twinklesocks like she's a prize he's won without trying, and says, far too calmly for someone who's just been groped by a woman in novelty pyjamas, "Jasper Corbin."

He even *smiles*.

Not a full smile, just a smug little curl of the lips, like this is going straight in his mental highlight reel.

I let out a noise. Possibly a laugh. Possibly a small internal implosion. "Right. Miranda. I'm your tenant. Thank you. For... the kitten."

He glances down at the ginger menace now purring into his sternum like she's claiming me as her owner. "She's very... assertive."

"Not usually," I lie, managing to retrieve her without incident this time. "She's just exploring. Territory. Windows. Freedom."

"Legs," he adds, eyes flicking to mine. "She seemed fond of licking mine."

I make a sound that might be a strangled apology and edge backwards, Twinklesocks tucked under one arm like contraband.

"I'll just—yes. Thank you again. Sorry."

I turn to flee, but he calls after me, mild as anything: "I wasn't told there'd be a cat."

I stop.

Not because I want to. Because guilt—and British social conditioning—physically won't let me keep walking.

I half-turn, Twinklesocks dangling under my arm. "It's… um. Two, actually."

His eyebrows lift, slowly. "Two."

"Stella said it was fine," I blurt. "I did ask. She said Jasper… I mean, you…. wouldn't mind. And she's the one who showed me round, and she approved the application and everything, so I assumed… well, you know. That she'd… mentioned it."

He doesn't say anything for a moment. Just stands there, lean and far too shirtless for a conversation about tenancy boundaries, while a faint breeze moves through his already infuriatingly perfect hair.

Then, at last, he nods once. "Of course. If Stella said it's fine…"

Oh no.

That tone. That very specific, deeply sarcastic tone of a man who's just been overruled by a woman he's clearly lost battles to before.

I open my mouth. Close it again. Nod, weakly. "Thank you. I'll, um. Go."

And this time, he lets me.

Because apparently, I have embarrassed myself quite enough for one morning.

I manage to shut the door behind me without dropping Twinklesocks or collapsing entirely. Just.

From the kitchen, I hear cereal being crunched.

I stumble in, still clutching the kitten like she's the last shred of my dignity.

SJ looks up from the table the moment I appear. "Did you find her?!"

I nod, holding Twinklesocks aloft. "Caught red-pawed, breaking into someone's house."

He gasps. "*Whose* house?"

"Our landlord's."

His eyes go huge. "She got into his house?!"

"She licked his leg."

There's a pause.

"She what?"

"It's not important."

He swings his legs under the chair, face aglow with awe. "Was he mad?"

"No."

"Did he shout?"

"No."

"Did you say sorry?"

"I said sorry *multiple* times. I was very British about it."

He peers at me, frowning. "Why are your ears red?"

"Because it's freezing out there," I say quickly, brushing him off. "Now finish your breakfast. The driver will be here in twenty minutes."

He groans dramatically and slumps forward, nearly face-first into his cereal bowl. "Do I *have* to go?"

"Yes," I say, pouring boiling water into my mug. "It's school. Not exile."

"It feels like exile."

"You're going to see your friends. You like your friends."

"I like *some* of them."

I pass him a stern look over the steam rising from the kettle. He picks up his spoon with the weary air of someone being gravely wronged by the national curriculum.

I remove the teabag from my mug and try to ignore the damp chill still clinging to my pyjamas and the ghostly memory of my palm making contact with a stranger's chest muscle. Repeatedly.

Nope. Not thinking about it.

Driver in twenty minutes. Lunch in SJ's bag. My sanity somewhere near the back fence with the traumatised shrubbery.

One thing at a time.

The bell over the café door jingles as I step inside. The girls are helping me unpack all the boxes we didn't manage yesterday but we agreed to meet for a coffee first. Get a caffeine fix in to build up the energy.

All four are already there, of course. They claimed a table by the window. There are mugs and coats and overlapping chatter... I can't help smiling at my friends when Bri spots me first.

"There she is!" she calls, standing to kiss both my cheeks and nearly knocking over her coffee in the process. "Our favourite Little Hadlow newcomer."

Amelia's next, wrapping me in a hug that smells of perfume and croissant. "You look... windswept."

"That's generous," I mutter. "It's been a morning."

Fi slides a fresh flat white toward the empty seat. "We assumed as much. You're thirty minutes late and you haven't rage-texted once."

Lizzie grins from across the table. "Do we need trickery or are you going to tell us everything voluntarily?"

I take the seat, wrap my hands around the mug, and exhale.

"Let me defrost first," I say. "Then you can interrogate me all you like."

I take a sip of the flat white, gloriously hot, mercifully strong, and hold the cup a moment longer than necessary.

"Twinklesocks escaped," I say flatly.

Fi lowers her mug. "Already?"

"Did you find her?" Lizzie asks.

"Yes."

"Where?" Bri leans in.

"Next door." I take another sip. "The landlord had his patio doors open. She invaded his kitchen."

Four mouths fall open.

Amelia blinks. "So you followed her into his kitchen?"

"No," I say, shaking my head. "I didn't know she was in his kitchen. I was crawling through the hedges. In the garden. Like a mad woman."

They're already smiling.

"In what?" Bri asks, far too gleefully.

I close my eyes. "A winter coat. Reindeer pyjamas, and... slippers."

Fi makes a strangled noise into her coffee. Lizzie actually chokes.

Amelia claps her hands once. "Oh, this is already better than I hoped."

I take another sip. "Has any one of you actually met Jasper?"

Amelia raises a brow. "I have."

That grin. The slow, smug kind that sets off alarm bells around the table.

Bri narrows her eyes. "What was *that* look?"

Lizzie leans in. "Did you forget to mention the landlord is hot? He rushed past so quickly om Bonfire night, I couldn't see."

Amelia just sips her cappuccino, not even pretending to be innocent.

Fi turns to me. "Miranda. How hot are we talking?"

I set my mug down with a sigh. "He is... hot as lava."

There's a squeal from Bri. Lizzie punches the table.

"Details!" Fi demands.

"Dark hair, messy in a good way. Golden streaks in it like he's been permanently backlit. Eyes that make you forget your name. Stubble. Muscles."

All four are now staring at me like I've been holding out state secrets.

"And he was shirtless," I add.

Bri grabs my wrist like we're about to take flight. "Please tell me you have a photo."

"Oh absolutely," I say, deadpan. "Because patting his pec wasn't mortifying enough, I obviously followed it up by asking if he could pose like a thirst trap against the fridge."

Amelia nearly spills her cappuccino. "Wait. You did *what*?"

I drop my head onto the table with a quiet *thunk*. "I patted his pec."

"You *patted* it?" Fi echoes.

"Not like I was checking ripeness," I mumble. "It was accidental. Reflexive. Kitten confusion."

There's a beat of stunned silence—and then Lizzie makes a noise like a dying kettle.

"Fucking hell," Bri whispers, clutching her chest like she's been personally blessed. "You groped the landlord's actual chest?"

"I didn't mean to! I was reaching for Twinklesocks and miscalculated."

"You confused tense muscle with a furry, little kitten?" Fi asks mildly.

I lift my head just enough to glare at her. "I panicked. My hand betrayed me. I have no defence except… maybe I'm becoming a hormonal cliché."

Amelia leans across the table, beaming. "We love this for you."

"I don't," I mutter. "I want to crawl back into my reindeer pyjamas and start again."

Amelia folds her arms, giving me *that* look. "Maybe it's time."

I frown. "Time for what?"

"To move on."

I blink. "It's been less than a month since the divorce was final."

"Yes, but you've been separated since summer," Fi points out, ever the rational assassin.

"And before that," Lizzie adds, picking up her croissant like a microphone, "when was the last time you and Sim-Sim even shagged?"

I nearly inhale my flat white.

"Excuse me?!"

"Serious question," she says, unapologetic. "Give us a ballpark."

"I'm not ballparking my sex life in a public café."

Bri grins. "So that long, then."

"I'm just saying," Amelia says gently, "you're allowed to notice an attractive man. You're divorced, not dead."

"I didn't notice him," I lie.

"You patted his chest."

"That was cat-related."

"Sure it was."

Fi lifts her mug. "To fresh starts."

I groan into my hands. "To public humiliation."

8

Away in a Basket

Jasper

There's the faint sound of voices through the shared wall. Nothing distinct, just the low murmur that says someone's home.

I grab the basket of bits I'd panic-bought at the big Asda in the next village and head outside. This morning's mad dash wasn't retail therapy, it was damage control. All in the noble name of being a good neighbour… or at least a half-decent landlord.

It's a few steps along the garden path to the annexe. I ring the bell and wait. I'm still not sure what to make of Miranda.

She'd turned up in reindeer pyjamas, slippers, and a panicked crouch like she was mid-espionage. Chaos in human form. But there'd been something else too. Something warm. Feminine. Unexpectedly delightful.

Enticing, if I'm being honest.

The door swings open.

But it's not her.

It's a tall, curvy woman I don't think I've seen before. She gives me a slow, deliberate once-over and a grin that says she's enjoying the view.

"You must be the landlord," she says.

"Jasper," I reply. "Jasper Corbin."

She extends a hand, all confidence and cheek. "Lizzie. Tenant's friend. Occasional bad influence. Come in."

Before I can protest, she's already stepping aside, waving me in like I'm expected—which, based on Miranda's face when she appears from the back of the flat, I absolutely am not.

Eyes go wide. A flush creeps up her neck.

"Miranda," Lizzie sing-songs. "You've got a visitor."

Miranda blinks at me, startled, guilty, flustered like I've caught her smuggling antiques or singing into a hairbrush.

She's dressed this time. Black dungarees over a stripy top, blonde hair in two neat plaits that make her look both younger and... still somehow dangerously distracting.

She is slightly less chaotic than this morning but still delightfully crazy.

I clear my throat, keeping my tone smooth.

"Apologies for the interruption," I say, holding up the basket. "Just thought I'd drop this off."

She watches it with caution.

"I'm not big on flowers," I go on. "They die in three days and shed everywhere, which feels like a pointed metaphor for most housewarming gifts. So instead—bread and salt. Traditional. For a new home. There's some kitten food in there, chocolate for your son..."

A beat.

"...and reindeer socks. For you."

I add a wink.

Miranda turns scarlet.

Behind her, there's a collective ripple—a sharp inhale, a cough that's clearly masking a laugh. Amelia leans gently back against the fridge, looking quietly delighted. Lizzie lets out a muffled cackle. One of the others gives a soft whoop. The fourth just beams.

Miranda looks like she'd quite like the floor to swallow her whole. "Thank you," she mutters, taking the basket as if it's timed to explode.

I glance at the others, whose expressions range from amused to predatory. From the general atmosphere, it's safe to assume I've been discussed.

"I won't keep you," I say, stepping back. "Just wanted to welcome you properly. In daylight, this time."

I get another quiet "Thanks" from her.

I glance at Amelia, the only one of Miranda's friends who I have met in the past. "Tell Ben I said hi."

"Will do," Amelia replies, grinning far too widely.

"Have a good afternoon, ladies."

I turn and head back out of the house, and just before the door swings shut behind me, I catch a whisper of Amelia's voice—

"See? This is why you always answer the door with lip balm and a bra."

***

The pool's already buzzing when I walk in—humid air, too much chlorine, and the sharp echo of kids' swimming lessons finishing up.

There are three lanes. The far left has a man floating on his back. The middle one's a slow crawl of elbows and effort.

Callum's in the third, the fast lane—our lane—sitting on the edge, flicking water off his fingers.

He clocks me as I walk over. "I was beginning to think you'd chickened out."

"Sorry, had to make a delivery," I say, dropping my towel onto the bench.

I climb in. Cold. Sharp. Good.

We swim ten lengths to warm up and I can feel the familiar enjoyment my muscles get from swimming. I'm not keen on the gym even if I do run on the treadmill quite often. It always feels like a work out, punishment for something. Swimming feels like a reward.

We pause at the deep end, arms hooked over the edge, water lapping quietly around us.

Callum nudges my arm with his elbow. "So. You met the tenant yet?"

"That was the delivery," I say. "Had to drop off a gift basket."

He glances over. "A basket?"

"Mm."

"What was in it?"

"Bread. Salt. Chocolate for the kid. Kitten food."

His brow furrows. "That's... surprisingly thoughtful. For you."

I shrug. "Felt like something a landlord should do."

Callum snorts. "The only other time you tried to rent out the flat you welcomed the bloke by telling him the bins go out on a Wednesday and not to feed the foxes."

I stay quiet.

"So?" he presses.

"There was a moment."

He raises a brow. Waits.

"This morning. I left the patio doors open after my run. One of the kittens wandered in."

"She came in after it?"

I shake my head. "No. She was in the garden. Crawling. Wearing a coat and... reindeer pyjamas."

Callum stares at me. "You're making this up."

"I'm really not."

He tilts his head. "And this moment... what did it include, exactly?"

I hesitate. "She may have... accidentally patted my chest."

"Patted?" he asks, biting back a laugh.

"I was shirtless," I reply, unable to stop myself from grinning.

"Oh mate. What's she like?"

I rest my forearms on the edge of the pool, staring at the ceiling for a second. "Bit chaotic. Hair everywhere. Talked to the cat. Dressed like she escaped a Christmas panto."

Callum looks amused. "So… a mess."

"Sort of." I pause. "But a warm one. Feminine. Funny. She blushes like it's a competitive sport."

"Uh-huh." His grin spreads. "And you're already smiling like an idiot."

I shake my head. "I'm not— It was a weird morning."

"And the basket was a totally platonic neighbourly gesture?"

"Obviously."

Callum tilts his head. "I didn't know she was also bringing a kitten."

"Kittens," I correct. "Plural. And I have *your* girlfriend to thank for it."

He frowns. "Stella?"

"Yeah. Apparently, she greenlit the whole feline operation. Didn't mention it to me, of course."

Callum doesn't reply right away. Just grins. Slow. Pleased with himself.

I narrow my eyes. "What?"

He shrugs, far too casually. "You know what, mate… I think you were right to suspect she's matchmaking."

I groan. "Unbelievable."

"You've got to admit, it's a pretty elegant move. Single mum. Cat chaos. Accidental pectoral fondling."

"I'm going to drown you in this pool."

"You won't. Because even all your money won't save you from prison."

I push off the wall and swim away.

His laughter follows me all the way to the shallow end.

We swim hard for another half hour—enough to burn off any lingering smugness on Callum's part. By the time we haul ourselves out, my arms are protesting and my brain's finally quiet.

Neither of us mentions Miranda again.

The showers are quick, functional. As we're lacing up trainers, Callum glances over. "You watching the Chelsea–Arsenal game on Saturday?"

"Was planning to. At home."

He grins. "Don't. I got offered a box."

I look up. "Since when do *you* get a VIP box?"

"One of the suppliers. Sweeteners. Thought I'd bring some of the lads from the village team. You in?"

I nod. "Yeah. Sounds decent."

"You can even wear that tragic old Chelsea shirt you pretend isn't cursed."

"Only if you promise not to shout tactical advice to the gaffer."

"No promises."

Just as we're heading out to the car park, Callum's phone rings.

He checks the screen and answers with a big grin. "What can I do for you, my love?"

We keep walking.

A pause.

"Okay."

Another pause.

"Yes."

We reach the row of parked cars, steam still rising off us in the cold. He unlocks his with a beep.

"Sure. Yes. Great. Love you."

He hangs up and shoots me a smirk.

I narrow my eyes. "What's that look for?"

"Looks like I'll get to judge for myself what this Miranda's really like."

I stare at him. "Why?"

He pops his boot open to place his bag in it. "Stella remembered Miranda's looking for work. I've got a project coming up, and I need Stella fully focused—so we figured we could use the extra admin help."

"We."

He shrugs. "Stella's idea, technically. Interview's tomorrow."

I just stand there.

A bead of water drips off my hair and lands on my collarbone.

"This has nothing to do with me," I say flatly.

Callum just laughs, slamming his boot shut. "If you say so."

"She'll be working for *you*."

"Yep. While Stella runs the project."

"Exactly," I say, pulling open my door. "So good luck to you both."

Callum leans against his car, arms folded. "You do remember she'll be there when you drop by, right?"

"I've no plans to drop by."

He looks personally offended. "You promised you'd look over the stuff for the FCDO project."

I wave a hand. "Not an issue. I can be civil."

Callum raises an eyebrow. "Because you don't fancy her?"

I give him a flat look. "I never said I fancied her. I don't."

"Right," he says slowly, like he's humouring a pensioner who insists their cat can speak fluent French. "She's not your type."

"She's not," I snap, a little too fast.

He holds up both hands. "Sure. You only had a *moment*... You never have moments with women. You have dates, hook ups. But no moments."

"I go for calm. Predictable."

"You once dated a woman who brought an iguana to brunch."

I point at him. "That was once. And the iguana was named Nigel."

He smirks. "You remember the lizard's name but not hers?"

I glare at him, shut the door, and start the engine.

As I pull out, I can still see him laughing in the rear-view mirror.

Smug bastard.

9

Fairytale of New Vibrator

Miranda

The second the door shuts behind Jasper, there's a silence so charged it might as well come with a warning label.

"Oh my God," Amelia swoons.

Bri clutches her chest dramatically. "He brought you reindeer socks."

"And kitten food," Lizzie adds. "And actual chocolate. This man didn't just turn up with a basket. He turned up with a gesture."

I blink at them. "He said it was a housewarming gift."

"Oh please," Bri says. "Bread and salt *is* a housewarming gift. Chocolate for SJ is thoughtful. But novelty socks? That's flirting. Polite, winter-themed flirting."

"It is *not* flirting," I say. "It's quirky. It's practical. It's—"

"Personal," Amelia interrupts, eyes gleaming. "It's cheeky. You don't give novelty socks to a tenant."

I shake my head. "It was just a kind thing to do. A neighbourly thing. He's being polite."

"You're deflecting," Amelia says, smug.

"I'm redirecting," I mutter, pouring myself a glass of water and pretending not to look at the basket again. "He's just being nice."

And yet. There's a flicker in my stomach I don't fully trust. A fizz. Nothing dramatic—just the tiniest flare of *maybe*. It's been years since someone flirted with me. Real flirting, not pub banter or Sim-Sim's tired half-compliments. This felt... different. Warmer. Intentional in a way I didn't expect.

"Tall," Lizzie says, counting on her fingers.

"Broad," Bri nods.

"And silently competent," Amelia sighs. "Honestly, if he'd handed me that basket, I'd have proposed."

"He knocked. He gave me a gift. He left," I say flatly. "That's not romance. That's Amazon with manners."

"He *lingered*," Bri says.

"He absolutely didn't."

"He lingered emotionally."

"Oh my God."

I lean against the worktop, sip my water, and try not to think about the way Jasper said *reindeer socks* like it wasn't ridiculous. Like it wasn't the softest, most unassuming way anyone's tried to make me laugh in months.

It was a good basket.

That's all.

And yet—

I glance down at the socks again.

They're red. Hilarious. Cosy-looking.

I do sort of want to put them on.

Still… I'm not dating. I'm not even thinking about dating. I've barely finished unpacking. My marriage is still warm at the edges. I've got a child to settle, a life to rebuild, and two kittens who think my dressing gown is a climbing wall.

No complications. No crushes. No topless, brooding types with good eyebrows and thoughtful baskets.

Still.

I may need to start brushing my hair before opening the door.

Just in case.

It's just after ten. The flat is quiet, except for the rhythmic whir of the boiler and the occasional sleepy grumble from one of the kittens, who've made a nest out of a laundry bag and refuse to be dislodged.

SJ fell asleep quickly despite protesting that he wasn't tired... at all. And I have a feeling I won't be far behind because this has been a lot. For now, the thrill of having a job is keeping me up.

I'm still half-stunned Stella even called... or remembered that I said I was looking.

An admin role, of all things. I hadn't considered admin—not really. My mum will have a fit if she finds out. With my degree, I should apparently be tucked into the archives of some respectable museum, gloved and whispering about pigments. But that version of me hasn't existed for a long time. And the truth is, I don't even know if I want to be her anymore.

A job in the village. Five minutes away. Flexible hours. Something I can do and still be here when SJ gets home. It's not glamorous, but it's a way in. A way *back*. Or sideways, at least. Something to do until I figure out what's next.

It's strange, really. I used to feel clear about who I was. I worked my socks off at Uni so I could land my dream job at the British Museum. I worked my way up to senior conservator quickly. I was even discussing publishing a paper with a colleague. Then I ran into Sim-Sim and my life took a different direction.

The lamp throws soft light across the wall—blank, still. The kind of magnolia that estate agents call "warm neutral" but which makes me feel vaguely like I'm living in the waiting room of a very polite dentist.

There's a stack of boxes in the corner. I've unpacked all the useful things—clothes, shoes, bras that don't dig in like they've got something to prove—but the rest remains untouched. Books. Trinkets. That weird clay sculpture SJ made of "the family," which looks like three potatoes having a standoff.

I'm lying on top of the duvet, book in hand. *The Duke of Thornbury's Sinful Bargain.* Old favourite. Tried and tested. One of the filthier titles in my collection—the kind I used to joke about hiding behind the toaster in case my mother-in-law came over unannounced.

Usually it works. Comforting filth. Escapism with a corset.

But tonight... it's not landing.

I read a line about a heaving bosom and a velvet tongue and immediately picture someone trying to lick upholstery.

I flip the page. Try again.

The heroine gasps. The duke growls something about propriety and punishment and my brain promptly swaps him out for Jasper—cool voice, unreadable expression, gently pulling on my ponytail.

I groan and let the book fall across my chest.

What is wrong with me?

I don't fancy him. I don't. I'm just... needy. Tired. A little emotionally dehydrated. And—yes, alright—it's been a long time since anyone looked at me with anything other than indifference or mild exasperation.

I close my eyes.

He really did say *reindeer socks* like it was a perfectly normal thing to give a woman you've never spoken to for longer than six minutes.

And then there was that tiny beat, right after he handed the basket over—like he was waiting for something. A reaction. A thank you. A smile.

I sigh and flop onto my side, shoving the book under the pillow. The kittens stir in their fabric cave and one of them lets out a tiny sneeze, followed by a deeply offended meow.

I should go to sleep.

I've got a hundred things to do tomorrow. More boxes. A school form I forgot to scan. Something's leaking under the sink and I'm ninety percent sure it's coming from the pipes.

But still I lie there. A little too warm. A little too aware of the shape of my own body under the duvet. Nothing urgent—just that slow, crawling feeling. Restless. Antsy. Horny, if I'm honest with myself.

I roll onto my back again and stare at the ceiling, willing my brain to stop picturing Jasper in a towel, which is ludicrous because why would I ever see him in a towel.

But he'd probably look good. Obviously. That's half the problem.

I close my eyes and try to focus on literally anything else. Bricks. Tupperware. That time I sneezed in front of SJ's head-teacher and accidentally peed a tiny bit.

Nothing helps.

There's a pulse in my belly now. Soft. Persistent. As if my body's decided, without permission, that it's ready to feel again—and that perhaps reindeer socks were the sign it was waiting for.

I sigh, tug the duvet higher, and slip a hand down, mostly out of irritation. If I get it over with, maybe I'll sleep. That's the deal, right? Standard biological maintenance. Like flossing. Just with slightly more enthusiasm.

Except... it's not happening.

I try. I give it a decent effort—the sort of focused, practical approach that used to work without much fanfare. Eyes closed. Breath steady. I reach for the usual images: hands, heat, pressure. The murky but effective greatest hits reel.

But my brain has apparently gone freelance.

Instead of something slick and sexy, it keeps coughing up mental snapshots of Jasper—not even undressed. Just him, standing in my doorway, basket in hand, expression unreadable but steady. And the way he said *socks*, like it was the sexiest thing in the world.

Not arousing. Not explicitly. But still there. Lingering.

I switch tactics. Try a little more pressure. A bit faster.

Nothing. My clit is stubbornly semi-aroused but too tired to give me the release I am hoping for.

All I'm left with is the creeping frustration of trying to light a fire with damp matches. The longer I go, the more it starts to feel ridiculous—not sensual, not freeing, just... stubborn. Like my body's rolled its eyes and gone *No, thanks; come back when you're actually in the mood*.

I groan and give up. Hand flung across the pillow, legs tangled in the duvet, heart lightly irritated.

So now I'm under-stimulated and annoyed. Excellent. All I need is a cramp and a moth in the room and I'll hit the bedtime hat trick.

I glance at the reindeer socks at the end of the bed. Snatch them up. Yank them on.

They're cosy. Smug, almost. Like they *know* they're part of the problem.

I stare at the ceiling and let out the quiet, exasperated laugh of a woman fully betrayed by her own libido.

I do *not* fancy Jasper.

I do *not* want anything complicated.

I just wanted a quick, efficient release and a bit of sleep. Is that too much to ask?

Apparently yes.

I sigh, sit up, and reach for my phone like a woman on a mission. If hands won't do the job, throw technology at it. It's practically modern self-care. Somewhere between moisturising and replacing your dish sponge.

I type *vibrator* into the search bar, already regretting what the algorithm's going to do with that later, and scroll past the pink monstrosities shaped like cartoon dolphins. I'm not after whimsy. I want results.

I find a nice-looking one. Slim, unthreatening. Quiet, allegedly. Rechargeable. £29.99. Sensible. Respectable.

I'm about to click buy when I spot another model on the side panel.

It has *features*.

Lips. Not metaphorical ones—actual soft silicone lips, apparently designed to "focus precision stimulation on the clitoral area". There's also a flicky bit, curved, promising to "target the G-spot with rhythmic pulses."

I stare at it.

It looks... capable.

Seventy-five quid. Which, frankly, is a grocery shop and a half. Or a decent coat for SJ. Or many other much more practical and necessary items.

I add it to my basket anyway. Sit there staring at the total like it's a moral test.

Then I remove it. Obviously.

I sigh again, open the group chat and type:

Me

Is £75 too much for a vibrator if it's got lips *and* a flicky bit?

I'd add "Asking for a friend," but we all know the game's up.

Amelia instantly reacts with a crying-laugh emoji. Bri sends a gif of someone being baptised in a river. Lizzie doesn't respond. Suspiciously quiet.

Two minutes later, my phone buzzes with an email.

***Subject:* Happy (Early) Birthday, You Deprived Legend**

It's a £100 voucher for a website called BlissfulBuzz.co.uk, which I absolutely did *not* know existed before now. There's a note:

I let out a laugh before I can stop it. Loud. Genuine. The kind that bubbles up from somewhere slightly ridiculous and completely needed.

I stare at the screen a moment longer, then follow the link in the email, find the right vibrator and click *Add to basket.*

Because why not.

If I can't sort myself out tonight, maybe I'll be better equipped by Thursday.

And if nothing else... it's good to have friends who know when to crowd-fund your orgasm.

10

Walking in a Kitten Wonderland

Miranda

I'm five minutes early, which is very unlike me. Normally I operate on a precise rhythm of *just in time, mildly flustered, apologetically charming*. But I couldn't sit in the flat any longer pretending not to stare at the clock. So here I am, standing outside a converted villa with the kind of front door that screams "money, but make it rustic."

It's similar to Jasper's, only a different shade of expensive, and without an annexe clinging to the side like a witch's wart.

That's the thing no one warns you about when you flee London for a fresh start in a countryside village—half the people here aren't locals at all. They're ex-city dwellers with perfect teeth and muddy Land Rovers, hiding their burnt-out ambition under soft knits and sourdough starters.

I knock.

Stella answers like she's been standing there waiting. Her hair's up, her outfit casual in a way that only expensive jeans and confidence can pull off. She greets me with a warm smile that somehow manages to be both matey and managerial.

"Come in, come in," she says, stepping aside. "Callum's just finishing up a call, but I'll take you through."

The house smells like expensive candles and good decisions. She leads me through a corridor of clean lines and quiet wealth, and I do my best not to imagine the state of my own hallway—which currently features a toppled cat tower and an empty cereal bowl.

We reach a door at the back of the house, slightly ajar. Stella knocks once, then pushes it open.

Callum is standing behind a desk that would not look out of place in a Bond villain's lair. He's tall. Not Jasper-tall, but still over six foot. Tattoos creep out from the sleeves of his T-shirt... black ink and muscle, just enough to make any woman swoon.

He looks up and offers a nod and a smile.

"Hi. Miranda, right?"

His voice is warm. Polite. There's a glint in his eyes; not flirtatious exactly, but not entirely neutral either. Like he knows something funny about the situation but isn't ready to share it yet.

"That's me," I say, offering a hand. He takes it briefly and then steps back.

"I'll leave you to it," he says to Stella. "You've got the better interview technique anyway."

He starts to move past, but not before turning back and, with absolute casual confidence, drops a kiss on Stella's lips. An actual kiss. On the mouth. Not long. Not dramatic. But definitely... intimate.

Stella swats him on the arm. "Go away. Let me do the serious part."

He grins—that grin you only get from someone deeply in love—and disappears from the office.

Stella shuts the door and turns back to me, a faint flush on her cheeks. "Just so you know, that wasn't wildly inappropriate workplace behaviour. Callum and I are... together. Which occasionally slips into the office." Her smile is wry, almost apologetic, before she gestures to the chair. "Right, shall we?"

I nod, still not quite sure what dimension I've stepped into, but quietly grateful that no one's asked me to define my five-year plan yet.

The walk home is shorter than I remember, mostly because I'm floating.

I got the job.

Well, Stella's exact words were, "We'd love to have you, if you're happy with the hours and pay," which I'm choosing to interpret as a job offer and not a polite hallucination brought on by the smell of Stella's fancy fig-scented diffuser.

The whole thing felt oddly easy. Like slipping on a jacket you thought you'd outgrown, only to realise it still fits. Stella and I went on like a house on fire. I can see us become friends, not just colleagues.

Yes, it's admin. And yes, it's not what I trained for. But it's something. It's *mine*. And it makes me feel in control of my life.

I'm halfway up the path when I catch myself grinning. Not just smiling: a proper toothpaste advert grin.

Maybe I've got this. Maybe things are turning.

I open the front door and both kittens shoot out like they've been fired from a cannon.

"Oi!"

Thor bolts left, a blur of grey stripes running towards the bushes. Twinklesocks rockets right, tail high and ginger fur bristling with delight.

I don't even hesitate—I yank the door shut again and dash after Thor, my coat flapping, boots thudding against the path.

I catch him under a bush three doors down, where he's attempting to fight a damp leaf. I scoop him up and tuck him against my chest, huffing. "You are going to be the death of me."

He meows like I've insulted his honour.

I march back, unlock the door one-handed and shove him inside. He promptly flops down and begins cleaning his shoulder like he's the injured party.

"Drama queen," I mutter, then spin around.

Twinklesocks is nowhere in sight.

My stomach drops.

Please not Jasper's house. Please not Jasper's house again!

I head off in the direction she ran, scanning the hedges, trying not to think about the last time she invited herself into his kitchen like a feline home invader.

And of course, because the universe enjoys a bit of comedy timing, that's exactly when the sky decides to open.

Fat drops. Cold. Immediate.

"Brilliant," I mutter, pulling my coat tighter and picking up the pace.

I scour the verges, poke around bushes, even peer into the bin area behind the corner shop like a woman on the verge of a very specific type of breakdown. No sign of her. I whisper her name, then hiss it, then mutter increasingly desperate threats under my breath.

Not a whisker.

By the time I admit defeat, I'm soaked. Hair plastered to my face. Socks damp. Coat doing its best but losing the battle. I'm freezing, sniffling, and one sharp breath away from crying in public—which I refuse to do, mostly on principle.

I trudge home, blinking away tears and trying to convince myself she'll come back. Cats do. That's what everyone says.

They have a good sense of direction. And apparently no sense of guilt, the furry little sociopaths.

I turn the corner onto my drive just in time to see headlights sweep across the front of the house.

Jasper's car pulls in behind me, slow and quiet.

Of course.

Of course he'd come home just in time to witness the full damp tragedy of my existence.

He parks. Steps out. Opens an umbrella and looks over at me.

We just stare at each other for a moment. Him, dry and calm. Me, drenched and vibrating with barely restrained emotion, looking like I've crawled out of a lake to deliver a warning about water safety.

I try to say something—anything—but my throat's too tight.

And then, from the left—the *left*, where I swear she did *not* run—a soggy streak of ginger fur bolts out of the bushes and makes a beeline for him.

"Twinklesocks!" I breathe, stunned.

She skids to a stop at his feet, tail up, fur wet, looking delighted with herself. He crouches smoothly and scoops her up with one hand. She immediately nestles in like he's her long-lost lover and this is all perfectly normal.

I blink at them. At her. At the wrong direction.

"I thought she ran right," I say, too tired to filter myself.

Jasper shrugs under the umbrella, stroking her damp head with one thumb. "Maybe she changed her mind."

I let out a breath somewhere between a laugh and a sob. The rain trickles down my neck, and I suddenly feel the full weight of it—the wet, the worry, the humiliation of the whole chase. He straightens up, still holding her, and gives me a look I can't quite read.

Something steady. Something that makes my skin feel too tight under my coat.

I step forward, arms outstretched. "I'll—erm—take her."

Twinklesocks promptly tucks herself deeper into his chest and lets out a tiny, manipulative purr.

"Oh, don't start," I mutter to her.

Jasper doesn't say anything, just raises an eyebrow slightly as he gently transfers her into my arms. She makes a token protest noise. One of her paws stays stretched in his direction like she's clutching at the love of her short, ridiculous life.

"Traitor," I whisper into her damp fur.

He offers me the ghost of a smile, umbrella still steady above us, as if this is all perfectly normal and not the climax of a minor Greek tragedy involving kittens and emotional instability.

"Thanks," I say quickly, cheeks burning. "Really. Sorry about her. And me. The... whole situation."

"It's fine," he says, that same maddeningly smooth tone. "She's welcome any time."

I let out an embarrassed little laugh, half-drowned by the rain. "Right. I'll just... get her inside. Before she develops a full crush and starts bringing you socks."

As soon as the words leave my mouth, I freeze.

Oh God.

Oh God!

Did I just imply that *he* has a crush on *me*? Because of the socks?

I did, didn't I.

I meant it as a throwaway joke—about the cat. But now it sounds like I've drawn some sort of tragic line between his gift of reindeer socks and the language of kitten courtship, and now he's going to think I think he's been flirting with me. With socks. Which... to be fair, I did think.

But he doesn't know that.

Or at least—he *didn't*.

His eyes narrow slightly, like he's trying to decide whether I'm teasing him or having a breakdown. And honestly, I'm not sure myself.

I panic.

"Anyway, thank you—sorry—I didn't mean that how it sounded—she's just really into soft textiles—bye!"

I turn around. I don't look at him. I don't even breathe properly until I've closed the door behind me and locked it like a person who's definitely not about to combust from embarrassment.

Inside, I drop Twinklesocks to the floor, peel off my dripping coat, and mutter, "You're the worst."

She shakes her damp fur all over the entryway rug and sashays off, smug as you like.

I groan and press my forehead to the door.

I've done that awful thing—the thing women are accused of: inventing signals where there weren't any, turning a perfectly kind gesture into some clumsy narrative about *meaning*, and now I've basically accused him of being into me.

Because of *socks*.

Fuckity, fuck.

I close my eyes and exhale slowly through my nose like I've just disarmed a bomb.

Next time I see him, I'm going to have to act completely normal. Just... unbothered and breezy and totally not like I've replayed this moment seventeen times and want to move into a cave.

And under no circumstances will I mention knitwear again.

11

Deck the Halls (with Fairy Lights)

Jasper

It's the third time this week I've been to Callum's.

I tell myself that's reasonable. He asked for my opinion on a project he's looking at—something to do with a Japanese investor and expansion timelines. We're talking strategy, not making social calls. It's work. Or close enough.

Still, I pause before ringing the doorbell. Not because I've got doubts about the meeting. I just... hesitate. Like my subconscious is trying to point something out that I'm not in the mood to hear.

Stella opens the door when I finally ring the bell. “You again,” she says, stepping aside.

“I’m giving Callum free consultancy,” I mutter. “He should be grateful.”

She grins. “Oh, he is. He has been the other two times you were here this week.”

“I’m efficient.”

“You’re lurking,” she says, but there’s no bite to it. She gestures down the hall. “He’s just finishing up a call. You can go through.”

I nod and step inside.

It’s warm, smells faintly of mulled spice and pine—and then I spot her.

Miranda.

Up a ladder in the living room, half-balanced on the third step, stretching up to pin fairy lights along the curtain rail. She’s got one knee slightly bent, arms reaching, and her jumper has ridden up just enough to reveal a thin strip of pale skin and the faint curve of her waist.

She’s wearing a pencil skirt. Black. High-waisted. The sort of thing most people don’t wear for putting up Christmas decorations but if it were for me, this is the only thing she would ever wear. It hugs her hips, the shape of her arse carved out in perfect silhouette. Unapologetic. Classic.

My brain stalls for a second.

I look away.

Then immediately look back.

It's like being hit by something you didn't see coming—except you did, and you walked right into it anyway.

She mutters something to herself, wrangling a tangled section of wire with an expression of fierce concentration.

I clear my throat. "Need a hand or are you winning?"

She startles slightly, glancing down. Her eyes widen just a fraction. "Jasper. God. You're very... quiet."

"So I've been told."

Her voice is casual, but her hand misses the next loop of lights completely. She fumbles, then overcorrects, and the cable knocks against the window frame with a faint clatter. Her face flushes. Not full crimson, but enough to notice.

Before either of us can say something ill-advised, Stella saunters in, holding a mug in each hand and wearing that expression that says she's just a little too observant for anyone's comfort.

"Well," she says, grinning, "you remember where the office is, don't you? Or were you hoping to supervise the lighting?"

I keep my tone neutral. "Just making sure Christmas decorations are in the job spec."

Stella's smirk doesn't budge. "I don't think Miranda needs you to fight her battles."

"Definitely not," Miranda says quickly. Too quickly.

I glance up—she's trying for cool and snarky, but her cheeks are still pink. Her fingers twitch as she reaches to anchor the lights again.

I raise both hands and take a deliberate step back. "Fair enough. No interfering."

Stella leans against the doorframe, clearly enjoying herself. "Go down the corridor, back of the building—"

I catch myself glancing again before I shut it down. Fast, before I show some physical signs on how much Miranda gets under my skin.

"Right," I say. "Office."

I turn on my heel and head down the corridor before I can embarrass myself or say something even more revealing.

Callum's waiting when I walk in. Arms folded, grinning because he can add one and one together to work out why there was a delay between the doorbell going and me sauntering into his office.

He doesn't even bother with a hello.

"You know we didn't need this meeting today."

I head for the chair nearest the desk and sit down with more indifference than I feel. "I thought we said we'd firm up the investor notes before you send them back."

"We firmed them up on Monday." He tilts his glass. "And again on Wednesday."

I shrug. "No harm in a third pass."

He raises an eyebrow. "Depends who you're passing."

I level him a look, but he's already smirking like a man far too pleased with himself.

"Look," he says, dropping into his seat across from me. "You're welcome to hang around. I can ask Miranda for some fresh coffee, since that's clearly what's keeping your calendar open."

I don't rise to it. I've known Callum too long, and if I show even the smallest crack, he'll widen it with both hands.

"Do you want to go over the numbers or not?" I ask, keeping my tone dry.

He grins. "Sure. But if you think I haven't clocked the fact you're suddenly *very* available for in-person chats, you're kidding yourself."

I give him nothing.

"I am doing this all for free, mate. I could be charging you an arm and a leg!" I remind him that I am only here to give him a helping hand.

Callum laughs. "Charge what you like, *mate*. But if you're going to orbit the house like a hungry crow every few days, at least be honest with me."

"It *is* about the work."

"Sure it is."

I glance at the notebook I brought, and flip it open just to give my hands something to do. "I don't have time to orbit anyone."

He tilts his head. "Right. And all these drop-ins—just good business?"

"Checking progress."

"You know there's email, right?"

I give him a long look.

He gives me one right back.

Eventually, he shrugs, lifts his tablet and taps it to life. "Fine. Investor notes. Round three. Let's get on with it, before Miranda leaves and you come up with a reason to 'check in' again tomorrow."

I don't answer.

Because I'm not entirely sure I wouldn't.

We work in relative silence for the next half hour—or at least, Callum works. I contribute just enough to keep up the illusion that I'm entirely focused on the spreadsheet and not, say, mentally tracking the sound of movement from the living room.

At one point, there's a faint rustle and a low laugh from Miranda—something quick and off-hand, followed by Stella saying something I can't quite catch.

Callum glances up at me. I don't look back.

Exactly thirty-two minutes in, the door creaks open and Stella steps in without knocking. The look on her face is pure mischief disguised as helpful admin.

"Just letting you know," she says lightly, "Miranda's heading off now."

The pause that follows isn't long, but it's noticeable. Long enough for me to register it.

Callum closes his laptop with theatrical slowness. Then looks at me. Stella looks at me. Like we've hit the climax of a play I didn't agree to star in.

Callum leans forward, elbows on the desk, expression unreadable except for the faint glint of amusement in his eyes.

"If you're planning to offer her a lift," he says casually, "we can call it there."

I don't blink. Just shift slightly in my seat and glance at the clock on the wall, as if I'm only now realising the time.

"I should go anyway," I say, stretching like this has all gone to plan. "My brothers are coming over for dinner."

Callum lets out a laugh. "You want a BAFTA for that performance or are you saving it for something with more dramatic range?"

Stella smacks him lightly on the arm. "Be nice."

"Why? That lie had a wobble in the second act."

I ignore both of them, tugging on my coat and grabbing my notebook. "Right. Well. Glad we cleared that up."

"Crystal," Callum says, not bothering to hide the grin. "Enjoy dinner with the brothers."

I walk out before either of them can keep going—and before I say something defensive that confirms everything they're already thinking.

In the hall, Miranda's just zipping up her coat. She looks up, a bit surprised. "Oh. You're done?"

"Yeah," I say. "Thought I'd catch you before you left."

She tilts her head slightly. Waiting.

I clear my throat. "Do you want a lift?"

Her eyebrows twitch upward. "Are you sure? I don't want to—"

"Of course," I say, cutting her off before she can wriggle out of it. "We're heading the same way. And it looks like rain again."

She glances toward the window, as if to confirm it—grey sky, heavy clouds, that thick pressure in the air that always seems to come just before it really lets loose. She nods once, fast. "Okay. Thanks."

Outside, the wind's picked up. Damp and cold. I unlock the car, open the passenger door for her without saying anything. She gives me a brief look—unreadable—before climbing in. I round the front and slide in beside her.

The drive is quiet. Not awkward, exactly. Just... still.

She fiddles with the strap of her bag. I keep my eyes on the road but I am distracted. The heater hums gently, cutting through the chill. I could say something—about the meeting, about the lights she was putting up, about anything—but I don't. Neither does she.

She shifts in her seat once, then again. Crosses her legs. Uncrosses them. I notice every little move. I can't help it.

As we pull onto our road, she finally speaks. Voice soft, almost like she doesn't want to break the air between us.

"Thanks for the lift."

I nod. "Anytime."

And I mean it. Probably more than I should.

I pull into the drive and kill the engine. She's already halfway out of the car before I've even unclipped my seatbelt, making a beeline for the flat with that slightly hunched, I-am-casual-but-escaping energy she does when she's not quite sure what to do with me.

I follow at a slower pace, locking the car behind me, hands shoved in my pockets. The air's sharp, damp with the threat of rain. We're both heading the same way—just with different doors waiting at the end.

She reaches hers first.

And then pauses.

Bends down. Fiddles with something. I squint—it's a baking tray. A large, slightly dented one. She's bracing it along the bottom of the door like she's about to shield herself from a domestic explosion.

I slow.

"What are you doing?"

She straightens, startled. "Oh. Uh... kitten containment."

I blink.

She lifts the tray sheepishly. "The kittens have worked out how to jailbreak. If I don't block the gap at the bottom of the door, they do this weird little pincer move and shoot out like furry missiles."

I glance at the door. Then the tray. Then her.

"You're building a metal barricade."

"It works," she says defensively. "Usually."

I nod. "Inventive. I'm impressed."

"I'm surviving," she mutters, crouching to reposition the tray. "Barely."

"You could've just asked for help, you know."

She glances up, surprised. "With the kittens?"

I nod, stepping closer, hands still in my coat pockets. "I could look into something. A proper barrier or... whatever would stop the Great Escape."

She gives a quiet laugh. "It's not really something you should have to worry about. As a landlord."

The word lands awkwardly between us. Precise. Distant.

She straightens, brushing a curl out of her face. "Anyway—thanks again. For the lift."

Then she opens the door just a crack, tray still braced in one hand. "No escaping," she mutters firmly, addressing the chaos on the other side like a worn-out nanny.

I hear a tiny meow, a shuffle of paws, and then she slips inside, guiding the kittens back with a gentle nudge of the backing tray. The door shuts quickly behind her with a soft *click*.

Silence.

I stand there for a moment, staring at the now-closed door.

She's right, of course.

Other landlords wouldn't let her have pets at all. Especially not indoor kittens with a desire to roam free. They'd worry about scratched floors and lost deposits and carpets that smell faintly of cat biscuits.

But I'm not just any landlord.

And she's not just a tenant.

12

I'll Be Home for Gay Porn

Miranda

SJ's off with his dad for the weekend. The kittens are snoring in their basket, their tiny bellies rising and falling in perfect synchrony.

And I'm on the sofa, yoga trousers around one ankle, a burnt-orange blanket trapped over my crotch, and a very expensive, highly rated, frankly overqualified vibrator humming away between my legs like it's auditioning for an award.

The one with the lips. And the flicky bit.

It's been twenty minutes.

Twenty. Full. Minutes.

The vibrator is warm to the touch now—not quite dangerously hot, but definitely the kind of heat that suggests it's been doing overtime without a break. I even dug out that ridiculous bear-and-twink porn from the deepest depths of the internet, the one with far too much oil and entirely too much chest hair, just to give my brain something to bounce off.

Still nothing.

I don't know what's wrong with me. I'm flushed, I'm tense, I'm swollen in all the right places. Everything's twitching and aching and on the edge. But it's the wrong edge. Like the build-up's all static and no signal. My brain keeps drifting. Overthinking. Slipping out of it.

One moment I'm watching the porn and the next I'm wondering if I remembered to put the laundry on. Then it's Jasper, out of nowhere—standing in the kitchen, rolling up his sleeves like some kind of M&S ad with attitude, and suddenly I'm all flustered and distracted and not in the good way.

I throw my head back on the cushion and groan.

"I bought you for *results,*" I mutter, flicking through the settings again.

The vibrator ramps up into something worryingly close to lawnmower mode. It buzzes against me with all the subtlety of a construction site, but still—*nothing.*

I twist my hips. Breathe deeper. Try to let go. Try to focus. Think sexy thoughts.

Just then, the doorbell rings.

I pause.

It goes again—*ding-dong*, bright and annoyingly chipper, like it knows exactly what I'm doing and would very much like me to stop.

I try to ignore it. Try to breathe through it. But the moment's gone. Whatever tiny thread I was clinging to has snapped. There's no sexy thought in the world strong enough to compete with a doorbell going off mid-lawnmower.

I groan, frustrated beyond all human measure, and yank the vibrator out. It makes a defeated little noise as I switch it off and drop it unceremoniously onto the towel I've been sitting on. I wrap the whole thing up in one quick, vaguely ashamed bundle and shove it behind the cushion like I'm hiding contraband.

Then I pause the porn—a still frame of the twink gasping with his ankles pointing to the ceiling—and pull my yoga pants up. Face smoothed. Dignity... left somewhere in the cushions, probably.

I march to the door.

Whoever this is better be bleeding. Or be on fire.

I swing the door open, ready to give someone a piece of my mind, and nearly forget how to swallow.

It's Jasper.

In a tight black T-shirt that looks about one accidental stretch away from becoming illegal, and cargo trousers that wouldn't be out of place in a 1997 boyband music video. He's holding a toolbox in one hand like some kind of rugged DIY centrefold. There's a stack of wood and a box leaning up against the wall next to him.

He looks hot.

Like, absurdly hot.

And I—I look like I've just lost a fight with a malfunctioning sex toy and gay porn film.

Brilliant.

"I'm here to install a barrier for the front door," he says, straightforward. "Something solid to stop the kittens slipping through when you open it."

I blink. Possibly twice. "Right..."

He shifts slightly—not impatient, just deliberate. "Also thought I could fence in the patio. Give you a bit of freedom to leave the back door open without worrying they'll bolt. Figured it'd make things easier."

He nods toward the timber stacked against the wall, then looks back at me, steady. No smirk. No flourish. Just calm, capable helpfulness wrapped in a frankly criminal T-shirt.

"Oh," I say, mouth already two seconds behind the rest of me. "That's... thoughtful."

He waits. Just giving me time.

Eventually, I remember how to open doors like a functional human and step aside. "Come in."

He ducks slightly to pass me—not that he needs to—and walks in with the quiet confidence of someone who knows exactly what he's doing. He smells faintly of sawdust and fresh air and something warm and clean.

I close the door behind him, heart thudding and immediately remember:

1. there's a towel on the sofa with my vibrator bundled inside and

2. my laptop is still paused on gay porn.

And he's heading straight for the living room.

I panic-sprint past him with a muttered "Sorry, mess, just let me—" and all but launch myself in front of the sofa, planting my body in the exact spot that blocks the screen. Casual. Very casual. Like a statue that doesn't want to die of shame.

Twinklesocks and Thor stir in their basket to the left, yawning and stretching as if they've had a long morning of doing absolutely nothing. Twinklesocks clocks Jasper immediately—and that's it. Her little ginger body's off like a bullet, straight to him like she's been waiting her whole life for this moment.

He crouches smoothly, toolbox placed on the floor next to him, and strokes her back with one firm hand. "There she is," he murmurs. "Good girl. You keeping everyone in line?"

His voice is soft. Fond. The kind of tone that makes ovaries sigh and women go weak at the knees. Twinklesocks purrs like she's about to marry him.

I stand there, arms awkwardly crossed in front of my chest, doing my best not to swoon. Because this—this right here—this image of him in a tight black shirt, crooning to a ginger kitten, forearms flexed and face gentle?

This may very well be more effective than the bear porn.

And then.

Then.

From behind me comes the unmistakable, echoing sound of a deep male voice growling through my laptop speakers:

"Take it, boy."

I freeze.

Jasper straightens up slowly, Twinklesocks still in his arms. His looks past me.

I turn, flowing his gaze, dread thick in my throat.

Thor is on the coffee table, gleefully pouncing across the laptop keyboard like it's a toy made for chaos. The screen's bright. Loud. Very much *not paused*.

And on it, a large, hairy man is enthusiastically rearranging a smaller, naked man's internal organs with a level of commitment that should come with a warning label.

For a few seconds, neither of us says a thing.

Then I lurch forward, scoop Thor up like he's contraband, and snap the laptop shut with a decisive *clack*.

Silence.

I turn slowly to face Jasper, cheeks burning, throat dry, humiliation leaking from every pore.

He looks... confused. And maybe a little stunned.

Twinklesocks is still curled in one of his arms, purring obliviously.

Jasper's free hand is lifted slightly, hovering near her head, like he's trying to shield her eyes from the screen.

It's... adorable.

And also completely insane.

He's quiet for a second. Then he finds his voice. "Was that... gay porn?"

I groan internally. Externally, I mumble, "Yes." Because honestly, there's no bloody point in denying it now.

Another pause.

Then he asks, perfectly level. "Why are you watching gay porn?"

I stare at him.

My mouth opens. Closes. Reopens like a dying fish. "I wasn't—I mean, I *was*, technically, but—"I take a breath. "It's not about that. In normal porn, the guy's usually quiet. Just sort of... there. Doing things to the woman. And the woman's expected to shriek and flail like she's being exorcised."

He says nothing.

I go on. Because clearly, I've decided now is the moment to bare my soul in graphic detail.

"I'm not really watching it. Not the visuals. I don't care about some random dick going into some random hole. It's just the audio. The voices. When it's two men, they both make noise. One of them always talks. Dirty. Deep voice, bit of growl, bit of moaning. It's... a turn-on. That's all... not that it actually worked this time."

I stop. Mouth dry. Ears bright red. I can hear my own heartbeat in my neck.

Jasper doesn't move. Doesn't smirk. Doesn't offer pity for the sad, lonely divorcee who needs high-production-value twink porn to get through a Saturday afternoon.

He just stands there, entirely still. His expression completely blank.

And somehow that's *so much worse.*

Because I don't know what he's thinking.

Not a clue.

He shifts slightly, then clears his throat. "Maybe I should come back another time. Let you, uh... carry on."

I stare at him.

"I mean," he adds, very politely, "I didn't realise I was interrupting. Sorry."

He crouches just enough to place Twinklesocks gently on the floor, and as he turns to leave, I swear he subtly adjusts himself.

Just a little rearrange in the trouser region. Barely there.

My brain lights up like someone's flicked a faulty switch.

Was that...?

No.

Was it the porn?

Or my awkward explanation?

Or maybe—

Oh *God*, maybe he's *gay*. Maybe that's why he spends so much time at Callum's. Not that there would be anything wrong with it. Except that Callum is with Stella, of course. Oh, maybe they have some secret thing, maybe they do a reverse haram thing?

I spiral for a good ten seconds—full internal PowerPoint presentation, complete with footnotes and sexual identity theories—before he turns back around and interrupts it.

"Why wasn't it working?" he asks, voice still maddeningly even.

"What?"

"The... thing. The audio. The... self-love. All of it." His brow lifts just slightly. "Why wasn't it working?"

And just like that, I forget how to breathe.

Because he's not teasing me.

He's asking.

Like he actually wants to know.

"I haven't had sex in a really long time," I blurt.

His brow lifts, just slightly.

"My ex and I were more just sharing a flat and... and I thought, you know, that's marriage. You get comfy. Tired. You prioritise laundry and work commitments and scheduling eye tests."

I take a breath. Bad idea. I'm mid-spiral now.

"But then I left. And the itch came back with a vengeance. Like some kind of hormonal zombie uprising. I thought, fine. We'll sort it. I'll fix it. I'll buy the bloody vibrator."

I stomp to the sofa, yank the cushion aside, and unwrap the towel with theatrical flair.

"There!" I say, brandishing the thing like a glittery, anatomical lightsabre. "Seventy-five pounds worth of high-tech vibration and *nothing*. *Nada*. I've had more success with bad dreams and an itchy tag on a pair of tights."

He blinks.

I keep going, waving the vibrator like it insulted my ancestors.

"I tried everything. Baths. Fantasies. Guided audio filth. And that bear porn, which is honestly very well lit. But whatever I do, it's like my orgasm takes one look, shakes her head, and swans off muttering, 'Not with that attitude.'" I pause, chest heaving. "Something's wrong with me."

Finally, *finally*, I stop.

Jasper hasn't moved.

He's still holding the toolbox.

I'm still holding the vibrator.

This is the worst TED Talk in history.

13

O Holy Shite

Jasper

"I can help you."

The words are out before I can stop them.

They bypass my brain entirely, leap straight out of my mouth, and hang there in the silence like I've offered to take my shirt off and solve all her problems with a well-placed thrust.

She gasps.

Actually gasps. Eyes wide. Gripping that bloody vibrator like it's a weapon and I'm the intruder.

Which, in fairness, I might be.

I hold up both hands. "Not like that."

She stares. No blinking. Possibly no breathing.

But I can't walk it back now. And I meant it. The second she stood there, flushed and flustered and practically vibrating with frustration, I just... wanted to help. Instinct, maybe. Or habit. Or something else I'm not ready to name.

So I keep going. Gently. Carefully.

"You're wound up like a wind-up toy, Miranda. Anyone with eyes can see it. Shoulders to your ears. Jaw locked. No wonder nothing's working. You're carrying everything—and holding it so tight there's no space left for anything else."

She doesn't speak. Doesn't bolt either. Just looks at me like I've stepped off a spaceship.

"I spent a summer in Bali," I say. "After I sold my company and the money came in. Didn't know what to do with myself, so I learned from a relaxation genius. Proper massage training. Not the sleazy kind. Real stuff. Therapy without expectations."

A pause. Just long enough.

"I could help you relax. That's all. Platonic. Therapeutic, if you like."

I wait.

Because it's her call now.

But she still hasn't run.

She looks torn.

Her eyes drop to the floor, then flick back up to my face, like she's checking whether I'm joking or dangerous or both. She opens her mouth. Closes it.

For a moment, I think she's going to say yes.

And then—quietly, with a small apologetic smile—she says, "Maybe just the cat-proofing of the flat... for now."

I nod. Not disappointed. Maybe even relieved. "Of course."

I clear my throat and make my voice as calm and neutral as I can. "If you ever change your mind, the offer's there. No pressure. No questions. No expectations. All professional."

She nods quickly, tucks a stray curl behind her ear, and doesn't quite meet my eyes.

I glance towards the front door. "Might be easiest to lock the kittens in the bathroom while I install the gate. Last thing I need is Thor wedging himself under a skirting board or launching himself into the hedge mid-build."

"Right," she says, grateful for the shift in topic. "Good idea."

She scoops up Twinklesocks, who immediately starts wailing in protest, full drama. Thor trots along behind them as if he knows something suspicious is happening.

I hear the bathroom door click shut, followed by the tap running. I give her the privacy. Start unpacking the box. Lining up the screws. Measuring the frame. Letting the shift to work mode settle me again.

It helps. Mostly.

Still—as I drill the first guide holes into the frame, I can't help but wonder if I've gone too far.

She was already rattled, barely holding herself together, and I just... offered my hands. Not like *that*, but still. There's a line between helping and overstepping. I'm not entirely sure I didn't cross it.

A half an hour later, the retractable gate clicks into place with satisfying ease. The kittens won't be flinging themselves into the driveway anytime soon.

I'm just wiping down the last bit of dust when I hear her approach. She's barefoot now, and the sound of her steps on the floorboards is soft, tentative.

I look up.

She's holding a mug. Steam curls from the top. She holds it out.

"Tea," she says. "Builder's strength. Figured you'd earned it."

I take it with a nod. "Thanks."

She leans against the wall, arms crossed—casual, but not quite relaxed.

Then, without looking at me, she says, "If I were interested—not saying I am—what would it entail?"

She delivers it like she's asking about garden waste collection.

I take a sip of tea. Let the question hang for a second, just to make sure it's real.

Then I look at her. "In this context?"

She nods. "Mmhmm."

I take another sip of tea, mostly to buy a second. Because this—this is where I should tread carefully.

It was easy to offer. To say purely platonic, no expectations, just help. But now that she's actually asking? Now that the idea is hovering between us like static?

It feels a lot less platonic.

"I'd keep it professional," I say, voice even. "Massage table. Fully covered. Light pressure at first, just to get your body used to being touched without flinching. Breathing cues. Stretching. Nothing invasive."

She glances up at that. I hold her gaze, steady.

"You'd be in control. At any point, if something didn't feel right, it stops. You say when. I'd check in, keep everything clear. Boundaries defined."

She nods again, slower this time. Still listening. Still deciding.

I take another sip of tea to hide the way my jaw tightens.

Because the truth is, this is probably a bad idea.

I've massaged plenty of people when I was in Bali, even a few dates when I was back in the UK. And once Geoff when he pulled a muscle in his back playing rugby. There isn't anything in it. It is just a massage. I can offer that to anyone.

But Miranda isn't just anyone.

And the idea of laying my hands on her—on that soft curve of her lower back, the tension tucked into her shoulders, the line of her neck when she tips her head back—it already has my pulse speeding up.

I could do it. Of course I could.

But I'm not sure I'd be able to do it without *wanting*.

And wanting is dangerous.

Especially when she's lonely. Raw.

I take a breath. Steady myself.

"If you were interested," I say, matching her tone, "it would be a simple back massage. Working out the knots... the tension. Just a way to let your body remember how to relax. That's all."

That's the lie I tell myself.

That's the bit I pretend I'd be able to stick to.

She hums, like she's thinking it over—but I already know she's not going to say yes.

Sure enough, after a beat she straightens from the wall and says, "Right. Thanks. That was just me being nosy, anyway. I'm not really... considering it."

Her voice is casual. Breezy (maybe a bit too breezy). She waves a hand, like she's brushing away the entire conversation, then disappears back into the flat before I can read her expression properly.

I nod to the empty hallway like an idiot.

"Right."

I stare at the tea for a second, then set it down on the windowsill and go back to the toolbox. Still a few screws to tighten, and then on to fencing in the patio. Just something to put my hands on that *isn't her*.

I meant what I said.

And I would've kept it professional.

But part of me is relieved she said no.

Because I'm not entirely sure I'd have managed it.

The village green's been transformed into a festive fever dream. Twinkly lights everywhere, children off their heads on sugar and seasonal adrenaline, and at least three men dressed as Father Christmas wandering around with wildly varying beard quality. Someone's playing Christmas songs through a too-small speaker that keeps skipping, and the mulled wine stand smells aggressively like cloves and regret.

Lucy is clinging to my hand with the determination of a child who has spotted a bouncy castle, a pony, and possibly the actual meaning of life.

She stops dead in front of a stall selling ornaments shaped like penguins in various professions—a fireman, a ballerina, one who appears to be baking.

"Uncle Jasper!" she gasps, tugging on my coat. "LOOK. The penguins are doing jobs!"

"So they are."

"I didn't know penguins worked! Do they have tiny lunchboxes?"

"Almost definitely," I say. "And a penguin staff room with fish biscuits and a very strict snack rota."

She stares at the penguins for a moment, then points to the ballerina one. "That one's called Lorna. She's in charge of the Christmas disco."

"Well, obviously. Look at that tutu. That's a penguin who knows how to party."

We move along, weaving between stalls selling handmade fudge, glittery candles, and several types of chutney that may or may not be legal.

Lucy skips beside me, cheeks pink, eyes wide, her bobble hat starting to do a slow spin toward the back of her head.

"So far," she says, very seriously, "I've asked Father Christmas for the big sparkly paints, the crown-making kit from the telly, a jewellery box that sings, and the magic scissors that can cut zig-zags."

"All sensible, useful items."

She nods. "And the Princess Aurora dress with the real swishy skirt. Not the one with the scratchy bits."

"Important distinction."

"Oh! And the rainbow pencils that smell like strawberries. But only if he's not too busy."

I glance down. "You reckon he's got room for all that?"

She shrugs. "If he doesn't, he can ask the reindeers to help."

"Delegation. I respect it."

We continue on, dodging a child with a candy cane twice his own size and a woman loudly describing a mince pie as "life-changing". A brass band strikes up *We Wish You a Merry Christmas* and it feels like we are smack bang in the centre of some Christmas special.

Lucy tugs my sleeve again.

"Uncle Jasper?"

"Mm?"

"If I ask Father Christmas for *something really big*... like... a castle... or a pony..."

"Ambitious."

"...Do you think he'll still bring it?"

I crouch slightly, straightening the hat that's now resting halfway down the back of her neck. "I think it's okay to ask," I say. "But sometimes Father Christmas has so many gifts to bring, he might have to cut some things of the list. So even if you don't get everything, you'll still get something brilliant. Because you've been excellent this year."

She considers this. "I *did* do good cutting at school. And I only cried that one time when we had peas."

"Strong track record."

She beams. "Okay. I'll say the castle is a *bonus wish*. And the pony's just in case he's got one spare."

"Very reasonable."

She slips her hand into mine again as we walk. The fairy lights blink. A snowman mascot collapses gently against a fence. Lucy begins humming *Jingle Bells* in a key of her own invention.

We've just passed the duck pond—currently frozen over and guarded by one extremely unimpressed mallard—when Lucy tugs on my arm again.

"Uncle Jasper?"

"Mm?"

"When are Daddy and Ivy coming back to get me?"

I glance down. Her face is calm enough, but she's chewing the corner of her mitten, which usually means she's thinking harder than she's letting on.

"Tomorrow," I say. "They'll be back for lunch. After their trip."

She nods, processing. "Are they having a grown-up adventure?"

"Something like that."

She skips a few steps ahead, then twirls, nearly slipping on a patch of frost. "Do they get to have pancakes?"

"I think it's legally required."

She grins, then keeps walking, content with the answer.

I watch her for a moment, then let my gaze drift ahead, to the shape of the house waiting for us just past the bend.

Theo hadn't wanted to go.

He never does, really. Not because he doesn't want to spend time with Ivy—he does, desperately—but because the man treats stepping away from the coffee house like abandoning a newborn on a roundabout.

It had taken both me and Geoff a solid week to convince him. Reassurances. Backup plans. Geoff had promised to be at The Kaisers Mug all day, every day, and brought out the big guns: "You're not the only person who can pour milk into a cup, Theo."

We'd also had to deal with the sacred ritual of Theo's "head waiter anxiety," which involved a laminated checklist, colour-coded notes, and a deeply suspicious look at the phrase *managerial initiative*. I think he fully expected the café to be reduced to ashes and espresso within twelve hours.

But eventually—miraculously—he relented. Packed a bag. Took Ivy off for a weekend without distractions. Just the two of them, somewhere with wine, silence, and sheets neither of them had to wash.

They both needed it.

Ivy, especially. She's been holding everything together with patience and duct tape lately. And Theo's the sort of man who forgets his own needs if you don't write them on a Post-it and staple it to his forehead.

So off they went.

And Lucy—to absolutely no one's surprise—had demanded to stay with me. She'd arrived with a pink suitcase, her favourite dinosaur pyjamas, and three separate bedtime books, all annotated with Post-its reading *NO SKIPPING*. She also gave me a lecture about brushing her hair gently, because "your man hands don't know about knots."

Which is possibly the best insult I've ever received.

"Home!" Lucy shouts triumphantly.

I catch up and ruffle the top of her hat. "Let's get inside before your nose falls off."

I'm halfway to unlocking the front entrance when the door to the annexe bangs open behind us.

SJ appears, hair wild, socks mismatched, face very serious.

"Mr Corbin!" he calls, urgent and breathless.

I close my eyes.

"Jasper," I say, automatically. "Just Jasper."

He ignores that entirely. "You need to come and help my mum. It's an emergency."

I turn.

He's bouncing on the spot now, full eight-year-old adrenaline, waving one hand like he's directing traffic. "One of the pipes in the kitchen *burst* and there's water going *everywhere* and she's saying things I'm not allowed to repeat and she doesn't know where the water button is."

"...Water button?"

"You know. The tap switchy thing."

"The mains?"

"Yes! The *main tap switchy thing*! Please, come fast or she might drown in tea towels."

Lucy lets out a gasp. "Is it a FLOOD?"

SJ spins dramatically. "It's *spreading*. There are puddles everywhere."

I scoop Lucy up before she can launch herself into the rescue effort like a very small, heavily accessorised fire marshal. She squeals with delight, clinging to my coat as I follow SJ at pace across the gravel path.

"It's a *real* emergency," Lucy whispers in my ear, eyes wide. "Like in *Frozen*."

By the time we reach the flat, SJ's already flung the door open and darted inside like a man on a mission. I step in behind him, Lucy still in my arms, and immediately clock the chaos.

Miranda's on the floor, half inside the cupboard under the sink, wedged awkwardly with one arm clamped around something beneath the pipes. She's drenched. Not mildly damp—*sopping*. Her ponytail is stuck to her neck, her jumper looks like it's been through a car wash, and there's a tea towel doing precisely nothing besides clinging to her forearm like it's lost the will to live.

"Don't panic," she mutters without looking up. "Everything's under control."

Something gurgles ominously beneath her.

SJ gestures grandly. "See? Flood."

Miranda glances up, clocking me and Lucy in the doorway. "Oh. Good. You brought an audience."

"You alright down there?" I ask, trying to assess whether she's stopped the leak or simply drowned it in sarcasm.

"I've created a temporary solution involving a hair bobble, a spatula, and blind faith. Don't question it."

Lucy stares, wide-eyed. "You look like a plumber princess."

Miranda blinks. "That's... unexpectedly flattering."

"It's the sparkles," Lucy explains, pointing at the water beading on her sleeves. "You're shiny and fixing things. That's princess work."

Before Miranda can reply, Lucy suddenly gasps again, dramatically enough that I instinctively tighten my grip on her.

"Look at the kittens!"

Sure enough, both cats are perched at the far end of the open plan like tiny, judgemental spectators. Twinklesocks is sitting on the cat tree, tail flicking, watching Miranda intently as if grading her plumbing technique. Thor is crouched beside the sofa, ears alert, tracking every movement like he's about to pounce on a leaking pipe.

"They've been there *the whole time*," SJ says, a little proud. "They like drama."

"I know the type," I mutter, stepping closer with Lucy still clamped in my arms. She's pink-cheeked, wide-eyed, and zipped up to the neck like a very short, extremely alert burrito.

I set her down and peel off her coat. Mine follows, both hung hastily over the nearest chair. She darts over to the kittens without hesitation.

"Right," I say, scanning the puddle situation. "SJ, would you mind keeping Lucy and the cats away from the wet area? Your mum and I need to sort this before it escalates into a full aquatic event."

SJ nods immediately, serious as anything. "Do you want to see my new Lego castle?" he asks Lucy.

"Yes! Does it have traps?"

"Obviously."

He scoops up both kittens—one under each arm—with practiced efficiency, then leads Lucy off toward the hallway. "We'll go to my room," he says over his shoulder. "I've got a blanket fort and stickers."

Lucy gasps. "I *love* blanket forts." And just like that, they're gone.

I glance at the spreading puddle, then nudge open the side door.

"Back in a sec," I say, grabbing my coat from the chair. "Just going to shut off the mains."

Miranda looks up from under the sink, one arm still elbow-deep in catastrophe. "Of course it's *outside*. Why wouldn't it be outside? That makes perfect sense."

"I didn't build this place," I say. "I just wrestle the stopcock."

She blinks. "That sounds rude."

I raise my eyebrows. "What are you? Ten?"

She snorts under her breath, but I catch the faint flush rising along her cheekbone. Flustered. Still a bit damp. Still trying to act like she's got the upper hand when she's half-stuck under a cupboard with a soaked sleeve and a cat paw print on her back.

I step outside into the cold.

The panel's half-frozen and stubborn as hell, but eventually gives way with a judder and a metallic creak. I twist the valve hard. Pipes groan in protest, then fall quiet.

When I return, Miranda's sitting back on her heels, shaking out her wrist. There's a streak of something unidentifiable across her forehead and her hair's doing that wispy, static thing from being both wet and annoyed. She looks like she's survived a mild hurricane and is now trying to style it out.

"Sorted," I say, peeling off my coat again and chucking it back over the chair. "The flood has been demoted to light damp."

"Thank fuck," she mutters, dragging her sleeve across her brow. "I was one dish towel away from declaring maritime law."

I crouch down beside her and peer into the cupboard. The pipe's still weeping, but no longer sobbing. A thin trickle pools gently beneath it.

"I think we can patch this," I say. "Towel, tape, wishful thinking. Should hold until we get someone competent."

She grabs a roll of duct tape off the counter and passes it over without ceremony. "We're aiming for functional, not pretty."

"That's been my motto since Year Nine."

She grins, quick and involuntary.

As I reach into the cupboard, her arm brushes mine. Just a moment. But warm. Solid. Enough.

"You know," she says, voice slightly steadier now, "I'd planned on using tonight to finally put the clean bedding on and watch *Bake Off* in peace."

"And instead, you got me in your cupboard with a wrench."

"Live the dream."

We work in companionable silence for a minute or two. She passes things when I ask—torch, cloth, tape—and occasionally mutters encouragement like I'm on *The Repair Shop* and about to cry over a broken vase.

When I lean back, the leak's been bandaged in what can only be described as plumbing cosplay. Not elegant, but secure.

I wipe my hands and glance over. "There. The worst of it's handled."

Miranda exhales. She slumps back against the cupboards. "Thanks," she says quietly.

I nod. "Wasn't going to leave you to do battle solo."

She gives a small smile—barely there, but real. A loose strand of damp blond hair has fallen across her cheek. Without thinking, I reach over and tuck it behind her ear.

She stills.

I don't quite move my hand fast enough.

"Stress like that," I say, my voice lower than I intended, "doesn't help with... tension."

There's a beat.

Then a strange little sound—half cough, half laugh—escapes her. She turns to look at me, wide-eyed.

I immediately regret everything I've ever said, done, or implied in my entire life.

Brilliant. Just brilliant.

Because now I'm thinking about the last time we saw each other properly. The conversation about tension and my hands on her tense muscles.

Bloody hell, Jasper.

"Right," she says abruptly, pushing herself upright and brushing her hands off on her leggings. "Tea? I'll put the kettle on."

She doesn't wait for an answer, just heads for the counter like it's a lifeboat.

I sit back on my heels and clear my throat. "I should probably take Lucy home soon anyway. Before she starts trying to redecorate your furniture with glitter glue."

Miranda's back is to me, kettle in hand. She fumbles with the switch, then says, without turning around, "I… I did think about it, you know."

I blink. "Think about what?"

She fidgets with a mug, still staring at the cupboard door like it's safer than looking at me. "Your offer… to—"

"Uncle Jaaaasssper!"

The word rockets down the hall a split second before Lucy herself does, bursting into the room at full speed, cheeks flushed and sticker in her hair. Twinklesocks barrels after her like a small furry missile.

"We played with the castle!" she announces triumphantly. "And I'm queen now because I had the most stickers and SJ said I could make the rules."

Twinklesocks launches herself onto me and promptly settles on my arm like I'm a deluxe cat tree.

I glance at Miranda. She hasn't moved. Her knuckles are still tight around the mug.

"Is that so?" I say, keeping my voice light as I adjust the cat's claws out of my collarbone.

Lucy nods enthusiastically. "But now we need snacks. For the royal banquet. And maybe something fizzy. But not the sharp fizzy. The nice one."

I give her a smile. "Tell you what, Your Majesty—why don't we head home and get you some proper dinner first? You can plan your next royal decree on the way."

She pouts instantly, bottom lip out like a professional. "But I want to stay! It's more fun here."

I reach down and gently lift Twinklesocks off my chest. She makes a soft noise of protest and latches on to my trouser leg the second her paws hit the floor.

"You can't come with me," I mutter to her.

Miranda, who's been quietly watching from the counter, says, "You could stay. I've got cottage pie in the oven. Plenty to go round."

I glance at her. She's casual about it, as if she's just suggesting a bin day or the weather tomorrow.

Lucy immediately turns to me with the force of someone who's just had her wildest dreams confirmed. "Cottage pie! That's my favourite!"

"It's got carrots in," I warn her.

"I'll survive."

Twinklesocks is now attempting to scale my shin.

I look back at Miranda, who meets my eyes with a look that's calm, unreadable, but not closed.

"You sure?" I ask.

She nods. "I'm not the world's best cook but my Cottage pie is legendary."

I smile. "Sold."

Lucy fist-pumps the air like a small, victorious knight and runs off to tell SJ, presumably by shouting at full volume from three inches away.

I reach down and detach Twinklesocks from my trousers again.

Miranda watches the scene unfold with faint amusement and says, "She really does like you."

I straighten up, brushing fur from my jumper. "I'm a likeable guy," I say lightly. "Semi-decent with plumbing. Pretty solid with cats and five-year-olds."

She arches an eyebrow, but there's the tiniest flicker of a smile.

"I'll go turn the water back on," I add. "If anything starts spraying again, shout."

She gives a dry sort of nod. "If it explodes, you're first to hear about it."

I head out into the cold again, flick open the stubborn panel, and twist the stopcock back into place. There's a shudder in the pipe, a faint creak through the wall. No immediate torrent of disaster, which feels like a win.

Back inside, I wait for a moment by the sink, watching. A slow drip... then nothing.

"All good?" I call.

Miranda's already crouched down, peering into the cupboard. "Dry," she confirms. "For now."

We don't say anything else.

Instead, we move—wordlessly—to the job of mopping up.

Towels are gathered, wrung, swapped out. A basin appears from somewhere. I find the mop and start chasing water into the corners while Miranda folds the least-wet tea towels over the back of a chair.

There's a quiet between us. Not comfortable, not awkward—just heavy. Like the room knows what was being said before Lucy burst in, and is politely pretending it didn't hear.

She hands me a dry cloth at one point, fingers brushing mine. Neither of us looks up.

The only sound is the soft squelch of damp towels and the faint rattle of the fan in the oven behind us.

I could say something. Ask her what she'd meant. What she would've said, if Lucy hadn't interrupted.

But I don't.

And she doesn't either.

We just keep moving—drying, folding, putting things back where they belong.

But there's an elephant in the room. Sitting there, right between us. Massive. Pink. Wearing a name badge that reads *"So, About That Offer..."*

And we're both pretending it isn't there.

For now.

14

O Come, All Ye Best Friends

Miranda

Dinner is noisy. Not the stressful kind, just the kind where cutlery clinks and the kids talk over each other and you realise, halfway through your meal, that your wine's gone and you have no memory of drinking it.

SJ points an accusing fork at Jasper. "You know Arsenal beat Chelsea this year, right?"

Jasper gives him a long-suffering look. "One match doesn't undo an entire legacy."

"Oh, come on," SJ says, clearly delighted. "Chelsea haven't won anything properly in ages."

"We won the Champions League in 2021."

"Yeah," SJ says with an exaggerated eye-roll, "*before I could do long division*. Doesn't count."

Across the table, Lucy's nodding along like she's following every word. She's not.

"I like the blue shirts," she offers helpfully. "And the shouting. Daddy always shouts at the telly when the blue ones are on."

"Same," Jasper mutters.

"There is very little shouting with Arsenal," SJ adds, grinning. "Just saying."

I snort because I know for sure that he and Sim-Sim have been shouting plenty this season because Arsenal is way behind. Then I turn to Lucy, seizing the lull. "What about you, Lucy? What do you like?"

"I like princesses," Lucy declares. "And glitter. And cutting paper into crowns. And my vet kit. And jelly."

I give her a respectful nod. "Strong choices."

"I'm going to be a princess vet," she continues matter-of-factly. "I'll live in a pink castle and look after unicorns. And sometimes hedgehogs if they're poorly."

"Obviously," I say. "Very inclusive."

"And Uncle Geoff is the queen," she adds, like that's a standard item on the royal staffing list.

I pause mid-sip. "Sorry. The queen?"

Lucy nods with great enthusiasm. "He wears the dress crown and the wings. He always does when we have afternoon tea."

Across the table, Jasper lets out a short bark of laughter.

"Oh, he absolutely does," he says, grinning. "It started with a tea towel and has escalated into full-blown theatre."

Lucy nods. "And he's not allowed to sit down 'cause he ripped the last dress."

Jasper shakes his head, still laughing. "She's not even exaggerating. Imagine Bruce Banner transforming into the Hulk."

Lucy grins. "But with a sparkly dress."

"Exactly," Jasper says. "You haven't lived until you've seen a six-foot-five guy, who plays rugby every weekend, having tea whilst wearing a sparkly princess dress."

I shake my head, still smiling. "He sounds like a great uncle."

Lucy doesn't even pause. "He is," she says proudly, then turns to Jasper and pats his arm. "But you're a great uncle too. Even if you don't wear the dress."

Jasper's face softens. "Thanks, Lu."

She shrugs like it's just a fact. "You always bring snacks. And you didn't get cross when I glittered your shoes."

"I had to go to a meeting in those," he chuckles.

"You sparkled," she replies with a dreamy sigh.

Across the table, SJ snorts into his juice. "Were they expensive shoes?"

"Handmade," Jasper says grimly. "Gold glitter. It did not come off."

I glance at him, watching the corner of his mouth twitch, the way he doesn't seem the slightest bit bothered by any of it.

And I don't know what to make of that.

By the time dessert is finished—two yoghurts, one crushed custard cream and something SJ insisted was a "palate cleanser" involving jelly—the energy starts to dip. Lucy's eyelids are drooping between bites, and SJ's gone quiet in that suspicious way that usually means he's either tired or planning something involving string and an ambitious pulley system.

"I should get her home," Jasper says, lightly brushing crumbs off his jumper. "Before she turns into a pumpkin. Or a glitter grenade."

Lucy makes a soft protesting noise but doesn't argue. She leans into him again, this time with a sigh that has bedtime written all over it.

Jasper gets to his feet, scooping her up like it's nothing. She tucks her head into his shoulder, already halfway to asleep, and I can't help but notice the ease of it. No fuss. No awkwardness. Just muscle memory.

I walk him to the door, arms crossed more for structure than warmth.

"Thanks for dinner," he says, voice lower now that the house has quieted.

I nod. "Thanks for the plumbing rescue."

"Any time," he says with a smile. "Though next time I'd prefer slightly less water."

"Noted," I say. "Next crisis will be fire-based. Much tidier."

He chuckles, then adjusts Lucy in his arms as she makes a soft snuffling noise against his shoulder.

I hold out their jackets to him and he wraps it loosely around Lucy to protect her from the cold, even if it is just a few steps.

"Night, Miranda."

"Night."

With SJ off in London for a birthday party-slash-sleepover extravaganza involving bowling, fizzy sweets, a round of Slush Puppies, and whatever sugar-fuelled chaos his dad's signed up for, I've been left with an evening entirely to myself.

So naturally, I spent twenty minutes pacing the living room trying to decide if I wanted to spend it in silence, in pyjamas, or at the bottom of a bottle of red, before settling on a fourth option.

Mulled wine. With backup.

I texted the group chat fully expecting at least two noes, one maybe, and Lizzie pretending she hadn't seen it until the next day. Instead, I got four yeses, one all-caps, and a gif of a woman lifting a giant glass.

So now we're here: five women, layered in coats, scarves, and opinions, strolling past twinkling lights and overpriced handmade baubles while the scent of cinnamon, sugar, and scorched bratwurst clings to the air.

"Why does everything smell like sugar and regret?" Fi mutters, wrinkling her nose at a churro stall.

"It's tradition," Amelia says, politely declining the mulled wine Lizzie offers her. "This whole month's basically a countdown to poor decisions."

"I think I've inhaled actual glitter," Bri says, inspecting her cup suspiciously. "I'm either festive or slowly choking."

"It's lovely," Lizzie says, sounding almost surprised. "Cosy. Like if Etsy exploded."

A brass band somewhere near the bandstand is attempting *All I want for Christmas* and failing heroically. There's a snow machine belching out something suspiciously like foam, and two kids are already fighting over the last light-up snowman hat at a nearby stall.

I take a sip of wine and let the noise wash over me. It's busy, ridiculous, and very slightly sticky. But it beats pacing my living room, imagining text messages I absolutely shouldn't send.

Lizzie leans in, smug. "So. Was the purchase worth it?"

I don't even pretend not to know what she means.

"I'm not reviewing it in a Christmas market."

"Oh, come on," Fi says, eyes gleaming. "We all chipped in. This is technically a product debrief."

"She's right," Bri adds. "We funded that orgasm. The least you could do is give us a star rating."

"I'm not rating it like it's a hotel stay," I mutter.

But I can already feel the heat creeping up my neck—and unfortunately, so can everyone else.

"Oh my God," Lizzie breathes. "You're blushing."

"No I'm not."

"Is this just about the vibrator?" Fi asks, eyes gleaming. "What happened? Did it malfunction? Did you imprint on it like a duckling?"

"I'm not discussing it here," I hiss. "There are children. That reindeer might be sentient."

"Spill," Bri says, sipping her wine with deeply unearned patience. "We paid for that thing. We deserve updates."

Amelia leans in. "You're being suspiciously quiet. Something went wrong, didn't it?"

I sigh. Loudly. The kind of sigh that's 70% regret and 30% residual shame. "Fine. It didn't work."

Four gasps. One horrified, one intrigued, one already laughing and one more sounding like a snort.

"Didn't work?" Lizzie echoes. "It had like... twelve settings."

"Fourteen," I say darkly. "And yes. I tried them all. My entire downstairs was vibrating like a spin cycle and still—nothing."

"That's tragic," Bri says. "I mean... mechanically, that's a success. Spiritually, it's a failure."

"Trust me, I know."

Fi tilts her head. "So what happened? You just gave up?"

I take a large sip of wine. "I was trying to get there. Had the towel, the mood lighting, everything. Even put something on for ambience."

"Music?" Amelia asks, hopefully.

"No." I wince. "Porn."

There's a pause. Then Lizzie cackles. "Oh no. What kind?"

I stare into my mulled wine like it might save me. "Bear and twink."

Fi squeals. "No!"

"I panicked! It was just the voices I needed, not the visuals—"

"Bear and twink?" Bri interrupts, delighted. "Is that like a wildlife documentary or—?"

"No! Gay porn. Hairy men. Squeaky bottoms. One of them growls. It's... hot."

Everyone dissolves into laughter. Except me. I am vibrating with humiliation—and not in the fun way.

"But the worst part?" I mutter, because I've officially lost the will to self-censor. "Jasper walked in."

Silence.

"No." Lizzie stares at me. "No."

"He *what*?" Amelia chokes.

"Doorbell went mid-lawnmower. I panicked. Hid the vibrator under a cushion. Paused the video. Opened the door. There he was—toolbox, tight T-shirt, he looked like a model..."

"Oh no," Bri gasps. "The porn was still up, wasn't it?"

"Well, not at first. I had paused it and strategically positioned myself in front of the screen."

"But?" Amelia grins.

"Unpaused by Thor. Bloody cat walked across the laptop." I still want to die at the thought of it.

Fi is crying. "That's the best thing I've ever heard."

"I nearly died. There was dialogue. Graphic dialogue. And Jasper just... stood there. Holding Twinklesocks. Looking like he was trying to shield her eyes."

Lizzie wipes her face. "I'd give anything to have seen that."

"I gave him a lecture on the sociology of porn," I say miserably. "And waved the vibrator at him. Like a wand of shame."

"Please tell me he ran," Amelia says, weakly.

I hesitate.

Bri narrows her eyes. "Oh my God. He stayed?"

"Even asked why it wasn't working," I mutter. "And then I told him I haven't had sex since... well, too long."

Fi fans herself. "Did he judge you?"

"No."

"Did he smirk?"

"No."

"Did he adjust himself on the way out?" Lizzie asks casually.

I go very still.

"...maybe."

Fi loses it. "You turned him on with bear porn and a trauma dump?! Miranda, that's a superpower."

I cover my face again. "I am never opening the door again. Ever."

Amelia grins. "Was the bear at least hot?"

"Amelia!"

Fi wipes a tear from the corner of her eye. "Honestly, you've outdone yourself. This is Oscar-worthy."

"I haven't even told you the worst bit," I mutter.

Bri turns, brows high. “There’s more?”

I stare at my wine. “He offered to help.”

“Help how?” Amelia asks warily.

“To relax me,” I say, and instantly regret the phrasing.

Fi nearly chokes. “He offered to shag you?”

“No! No. Not like that.” I wave a hand, nearly sloshing my wine. “He said he’s trained. Massage therapy. From a summer in Bali. Pressure points and all that stuff—not the dodgy kind.”

The group goes silent for half a beat.

Then Lizzie squints. “Wait… is that true? Is he actually trained, or is that just what hot men say before your knickers disappear?”

“I don’t know!” I say, exasperated. “He was so… calm about it. Like offering a cup of tea. But for… trauma.”

Bri nods sagely. “I mean, if someone offered me a trauma massage, I’d say yes and see what got released first—the knot in my shoulder or my orgasm.”

Amelia frowns. “But why would he do that? Just out of the goodness of his… suspiciously toned arms?”

“He said I seemed tense,” I say flatly.

Fi snorts. “What gave it away? The constant frown or the shoulders up around your ears?”

I bury my face in my scarf. “This was a mistake. I should’ve stayed home and joined a convent.”

“Too late,” Lizzie says, grinning. “You’ve got us—and possibly a tantric handyman slash landlord with a saviour complex.”

Bri nudges me with an elbow. "But are you... actually considering it?"

I choke on my mulled wine. "Of course not."

"Really?" Fi raises a brow. "I would."

"If I need a massage, I'll pay someone," I say primly. "Someone whose qualifications are framed on a wall, not wedged into the waistband of their cargo trousers."

Lizzie hums. "But would they be as... motivated?"

I shoot her a look. "He wasn't trying to sleep with me. He was being... annoyingly sincere."

"Exactly," Amelia says. "Which, weirdly, is kind of worse. Like, if he'd been sleazy about it, you could've just rolled your eyes and kicked him out."

"But instead," Bri says, eyes glittering, "he looked at you, saw a slightly panicked yoga ball and thought, 'I know what this woman needs—platonic tension relief.'"

Fi stifles a giggle. "Honestly? Sounds like a gift."

"Oh, come on," I mutter. "You really think letting Jasper Corbin manhandle me is a good idea?"

They all exchange looks.

Then, in eerie unison: "Yes."

"Right. That's enough about me." I glare into my wine like it personally betrayed me. "Someone please change the subject before I fling myself into the nearest snow machine."

There's a beat of silence.

Then Amelia clears her throat. "Well... if we're doing big revelations tonight..."

We all turn.

She bites her lip, cheeks pink from either the cold or nerves, and places a protective hand over her coat zip. “I’m pregnant.”

The silence stretches for a second.

Then Lizzie gasps. Fi squeals. Bri shrieks and almost spills her drink on a foam-smeared child walking past.

“You’re what?!” I say, laughing as the others descend on her. “You’re pregnant?!”

Amelia grins sheepishly as we all pile in, arms around her, awkward in coats and gloves. “It was a bit of a surprise. Not exactly on our to do list. But... yeah. Me and Ben are happy. Shocked. But happy.”

“Oh my God! I’m finally going to be an aunt.” Fi’s practically vibrating. “Do you know how far?”

“Just over ten weeks. We were going to wait a bit longer before telling everyone, but—” she shrugs, misty-eyed, “this felt like a good night.”

Bri clutches her arm. “You’ve just made the Christmas market iconic.”

We all cheer. There’s more hugging. A lot of exclaiming. I wipe my eyes, half-blaming the cold. And when someone suggests another round of mulled wine, we all agree (except for Amelia, of course) without even pretending to hesitate.

And just like that, the air changes, from teasing to tender. Because whatever else is happening, whatever vibrating chaos or awkward tension we’ve got going on, we’re still here. Together.

And that counts for something.

15

We Three Brothers of Whisky and Regret

Jasper

The steak hisses in the pan, the sizzle loud enough that I have to tilt my head away from the phone propped on the kitchen windowsill.

"Are you burning something again?" Geoff's voice crackles through the speaker.

"It's medium-rare," I say flatly.

Theo snorts from his little square on the screen. "In Jasper-speak, that's one step above cremation."

I flip the steak and hold up my free hand. "Perfect timing. It's artistry, actually."

"You're cooking a single steak at eight p.m.," Geoff says. "That's not artistry. That's bleak."

"Says the man who once ate leftover lasagne straight from the dish with a spatula," I mutter, grabbing the butter.

Geoff raises both hands. "Low point. I admit it."

Theo grins, but there's something softer about him tonight. He's lounging on his sofa, hoodie slightly skewed, hair still damp. Ivy's probably just out of frame. Lucy's well into bedtime by now. It's strange, seeing him settled like this. Like he's properly landed.

"I still can't believe we're not doing a family Christmas this year," I say, nudging the pan off the heat.

"Blame the parentals," Geoff replies. "Ditching us for bingo nights and rum punches during Christmas of all times!"

Theo lifts his mug in a sort of tired toast. "Mum said she needed 'a break from the cold and something turquoise'. Dad just nodded and booked the cruise."

"They literally live on an island," I mutter. "Guernsey has turquoise."

"Not Caribbean turquoise," Geoff says. "That's warmer. And comes with butlers."

"Honestly, I'm fine with it," Theo adds. "Means I don't have to cart Lucy and a mountain of plastic to St Peter Port. We get to do our own thing this year."

"And," I say, giving him a look, "you get your first Christmas with Ivy."

Theo tries to hide the smile and fails. "Yeah."

"Look at him," Geoff says. "All cosy domestic. Practically glowing."

"Shut up."

"Still dragging out the in-person introduction, then?" I ask, slicing into the steak.

Theo winces. "Not dragging. Just... strategically postponing."

"Because of Mum?"

"Because of Mum," Theo confirms. "She's like Guernsey society in a cashmere cardigan. I love her, but I'm not risking Ivy getting the full interrogation just yet."

"She's met her on video though, right?" Geoff asks.

Theo nods. "Once. Mum asked if she was a vegetarian and then offered her that weird rabbit stew recipe."

I groan. "The one with the sherry glaze?"

"Yep. Ivy thought it was a joke. I didn't have the heart to correct her."

Geoff grins. "I mean, technically, it is a family heirloom. Just not a particularly good one."

"I just want things to be calm," Theo says. "Ivy's happy. Lucy's settled. No need to go poking the bear in a Monsoon blouse."

I take another bite of steak, chewing slowly. "So what about you, Geoff? Any chance of you popping over for a day or two?"

He shakes his head. "Can't. Got roped into some fancy Christmas Day shoot in New York."

"Wait," I frown. "You're flying to New York on Christmas Day?"

Geoff pulls a face. "Christmas Eve actually. Some rich wanker wants me to capture 'natural, candid magic' with his genetically blessed children and their Labradoodle in a five-storey townhouse in Brooklyn. I'll be knee-deep in artificial snow and designer tantrums by breakfast. I'll be back after Boxing Day."

Theo raises a brow. "I thought you hated doing that kind of stuff."

"I do," Geoff says bluntly. "It's soulless, staged nonsense. And the dads always want their watches in shot. Honestly, I'm thinking of chucking it in altogether."

That draws a beat of silence.

"You're serious?" I ask.

He nods. "I've done alright. Been smart with the money, invested early, didn't blow it all on sports cars and nonsense. I could quit tomorrow and live off the portfolio." He pauses. "Might even be better for my mental welfare."

Theo lets out a low whistle. "So why haven't you?"

Geoff shrugs. "Maybe I needed one more Christmas covered in fake snow and sequin rage to finally tip the scales."

I lean against the counter, swirling the whisky in my glass. "Well. When you do retire, I'll be right there with you. We'll start a podcast. Call it *Men Who've Had Enough*."

"You joke," Geoff says, "but I'd do it. Come with me to New York. We can drink overpriced cocktails and heckle Father Christmas in Central Park."

I laugh. "Tempting. But no."

"Come on. Better than sitting around here eating a steak for one. You are getting broodier by the day. A break would do you good."

"Maybe," I say. "But I've got no desire to celebrate Christmas in a hotel room surrounded by over-decorated lobby trees and strangers in matching pyjamas."

Geoff tilts his head. "Fair. But you really want to spend it alone?"

"Don't start," I mutter. "I'm not joining your reindeer-papped misery tour. Christmas Day will be me and a nice steak."

Theo shifts in his seat. "Well, look. If you don't want to sit around sulking in your flat with nothing but leftover steak and self-pity for company, at least come to ours for Boxing Day."

I glance up.

"We bought enough food to feed a small militia," he continues. "Lucy will be knee-deep in wrapping paper and unicorn slime. You might as well be fed while being forcibly included in a tea party."

Geoff grins. "Sounds festive. And mildly terrifying."

"It's a deal," I say. "Thanks."

Theo lifts his mug. "Good. One proper roast and we'll call it even."

"Until next year," I add. "We'll do a proper family Christmas back in Guernsey. Full on turkey Christmas dinner, bad crackers, Mum judging our life choices from behind a sherry glass."

"Sounds horrifying," Geoff says. "I'm in."

"Same," Theo echoes. "I'll bring the Gaviscon."

We all raise our drinks in a slightly chaotic toast, then the call fizzles out with the usual chorus of sarcastic goodbyes and one last jab from Geoff about my cooking.

The kitchen falls quiet again.

I finish the last bite of dinner, rinse the plate, and load it into the dishwasher.

That's when the doorbell rings.

I pause, wiping my hands on a tea towel. It's late. Unexpected.

I head to the door, wondering who that could be, and find Miranda looking at me.

She's standing on the step in her coat, cheeks pink, hair a little windswept, and her expression somewhere between determined and slightly giddy.

She grins. "I accept your offer."

I blink. "...My offer?"

"To help me relax." She gives a small flourish, like she's presenting a prize on a questionable game show. "You remember. From the world's most mortifying conversation."

I narrow my eyes. "Are you drunk?"

She holds up a finger. "Not drunk. Tipsy. That fine line where your middle-class filter slips just enough for you to act on things you actually want."

I cross my arms. "Uh-huh."

"To prove it," she says, stepping back with exaggerated precision, "I shall now walk in a perfectly straight line."

And she does—or tries to. It's not exactly straight. More... determinedly wobbly. But she makes it to the end of the path, spins neatly on the spot, and throws her arms wide.

"Ta-da. Still legally upright."

I lean against the doorframe. "And this spontaneous sobriety demonstration is because...?"

"I'm saying yes." She returns to the step, chin up. "To the massage."

I raise a brow. "Now?"

She shrugs. "Why not? You said no pressure, no expectations. And honestly, it's either let you knead the stress out of me, or go home and alphabetise the spice rack in quiet despair."

I pause, watching her. "You're sure?"

She lets out a breath. "Absolutely. I'm going mental. I keep catching myself yelling at inanimate objects. Yesterday I told the kettle to pull itself together."

A laugh escapes me before I can help it.

"But," she adds quickly, "at mine. I'm not doing this in your flat. I already had to perform a bloody sobriety test. I'm not adding 'wandering the drive in my dressing gown' to the list."

"Fair," I say. "Your flat it is."

She hesitates. "Right. So... how naked are we talking?"

I arch an eyebrow. "You'll be covered the whole time. Always. I won't see anything. Promise."

She nods, but her nerves are clearly creeping in. "You're really sure this isn't weird? I mean, it's weird. But it's not *weird* weird?"

"If you don't want to—"

"No, no," she rushes. "Just—if *you* don't want to. I mean, maybe this is mad. It's probably mad. Maybe I should just go back inside and—"

"Miranda."

She stops.

"Go get ready," I say gently. "I'll grab the table and be there in ten."

Her shoulders drop with a half-laugh, half-sigh of relief. "Okay. Okay."

And before she can overthink it again, she turns on her heel and heads back across the path, muttering something about clean towels and lighting that doesn't make her look like a corpse.

I stand in the doorway for a second, then run a hand through my hair and head inside.

What the hell am I doing?

16

All I Want for Christmas Is an Orgasm

Miranda

I strip off so fast I nearly trip over my own jeans.

Underwear stays on. I'm not completely deranged. But I do swap my jumper and trousers for a soft bathrobe that feels like a hug I don't deserve. Then I stare at myself in the mirror and immediately hate everything.

I undo the ponytail so it falls around my shoulders—too fluffy. I smooth it back into something sleeker—too harsh. Then I compromise by doing what I always do when I've run out of options: messy bun. Slightly chaotic. Arguably charming. Matches the rest of my personality.

The kittens are watching from the bed like they're rating my life choices out of ten. Thor yawns. Twinklesocks blinks in slow disapproval.

"Oh hush," I mutter, digging around in the bathroom cabinet for something vaguely spa-like. "You've both licked your own bums in front of houseguests. You don't get to judge."

I spritz a little perfume into the air like it'll fix the general air of panic, then glance down at my toes. Chipped polish. Disaster.

Do I have time to paint them?

I crouch, rummaging in the basket under the sink for that emergency nail varnish I'm pretty sure expired back when the Princess of Wales was still Kate Middleton—

The doorbell rings.

I freeze.

Twinklesocks leaps off the bed and bolts for the door like she's about to collect a prize.

Fuck.

He's here.

I open the door with a kind of breezy casualness but I am not sure he is buying it.

Jasper stands there holding a large foldable massage table like it's the most normal thing in the world. He looks calm. Infuriatingly so. Meanwhile, I'm half-dressed, half-panicking, and fully aware that I haven't exhaled properly in about ten minutes.

"Evening," he says, voice low and steady.

I try for a smile and probably land somewhere between polite and electrocuted. “Come in.”

He steps inside, gaze flicking around like he’s clocking exits and soft furnishings, then glances back at me.

“So… the living room?” I say, gesturing vaguely. “Feels like the least risky option.”

“Living room works,” he agrees, following me through.

The kittens are already there—naturally. Twinklesocks is perched on the arm of the sofa, eyes fixed on Jasper like she’s been waiting to pounce. Thor is lying on his back under the coffee table, contemplating the ceiling with philosophical intensity.

Jasper sets the table down and starts unfolding it without comment. Calm, capable, quietly professional. The kind of man who could probably deliver bad news while simultaneously fixing your sink and keeping your grandmother calm.

Twinklesocks trots straight over and headbutts his leg.

“Hey gorgeous,” he murmurs, crouching to greet her. She purrs, tail flicking once, then hops onto the sofa and settles like a tiny, furry chaperone.

Once the table’s up and adjusted, he pulls out a small speaker and scrolls through his phone. A few seconds later, soft, spa-adjacent piano music floats through the room. Not too cheesy. Not too romantic. Just the right side of safe.

Then he turns to me, pulling two small candles from his pockets. “Final decision before we begin. Lemony or flowery?”

I blink. “Lemony.”

He nods, sets the other aside, and lights the wick. The sharp, clean scent starts to cut through my nerves—like someone's trying to disinfect the atmosphere.

I wrap my arms around myself, suddenly very aware of every thread of my bathrobe.

He looks over again, voice gentle. "Ready when you are."

I nod, throat dry.

Then I step towards the table, heart pounding loud enough to drown out the piano.

Getting onto the table turns out to be less "elegant spa client" and more "panicked squirrel trying to board a kayak."

"Right," I say, eyeing the table like it's about to challenge me to a duel. "So I just…?"

Jasper gives a small nod and steps back, very deliberately turning away. "There's a cover in the middle—just slip under it. Take off the robe, keep your underwear on. I won't look."

"Better not," I mutter, already undoing the tie and trying to keep some level of dignity as I shuffle towards the table like a contestant in a deeply unglamorous reality show.

Twinklesocks watches with interest from the sofa.

I manage to shrug out of the robe without strangling myself, then quickly dive under the sheet like it's a security blanket and the floor is lava.

Jasper waits a beat. "Ready?"

"Define ready," I mutter from under the linen, one leg still tangled and very much not where it should be.

There's an ungainly pause as I try to hoist myself onto the table. My foot slips. My knee knocks the edge. I let out a sound like a startled badger.

"Careful," Jasper says, not moving but definitely trying not to laugh.

"I *am* careful," I say, now half on the table, half flailing, fully betrayed by cotton.

Eventually, with a groan, a flop, and an accidental elbow to the face-rest, I get myself into position. Facedown, covered, and praying he didn't see as much as I fear.

"I'm in," I mumble into the padded hole. "I'm all yours." I regret the words the minute they are out.

Behind me, there's a very quiet chuckle. "Alright then. Close your eyes and try to relax."

The first touch is light.

Just his hands—warm, steady—pressing gently onto the towel covering my back. No movement yet. Just weight. Intentional. Anchoring.

And yet somehow, my breath stutters.

He starts slow. No oil. No digging in. Just smooth, gliding pressure through the fabric—up my spine, down again. Over my shoulders. His thumbs pause at the base of my neck, where tension clings like guilt. He presses, not hard, but deep enough to make something unravel.

I exhale. A long, quiet sigh that tries not to sound too much like relief.

He says nothing. No small talk. No awkward commentary. Just quiet music, the faint scent of lemon, and his hands moving with maddening patience.

I close my eyes.

It's fine. This is fine.

Just a massage. From a friend. A very attractive, unnecessarily competent friend who smells like soap and man and is currently pressing into the sore spot under my shoulder blade with surgeon-level precision.

I shift slightly and his hand adjusts with me, never straying. Always respectful. But still—oh, fuck, still—

How is this so hot?

Jasper's touch isn't demanding. It's not even particularly sexual. But it's attentive. Focused. Like he's listening with his fingers.

My skin tingles.

Stop it.

My thighs press together under the sheet, instinctively, embarrassingly. I try to relax. Breathe deeper. Pretend my mind isn't staging an entirely inappropriate one-woman show inside my head.

His hands shift lower, to the middle of my back, and then—slowly—he peels back the towel just enough to expose my shoulder blades. I freeze for half a second.

Then he speaks, softly: "Just this bit, if that's okay."

God. Even his voice is considerate.

"Yes," I mumble into the face cradle. "Fine. Yep. All good." The scent of whatever oil he is using is engulfing me.

My bra strap is moved with the most delicate precision, and then his fingers are there—skin on skin now. Kneading, sweeping, gliding over knots I didn't know I had. He finds the one under my right shoulder blade and circles it gently, coaxing it loose.

I actually groan.

Out loud.

A horrible, involuntary, low little noise that sounds like I'm auditioning for a very different kind of massage.

Jasper doesn't comment.

Of course he doesn't. Because he's a grown-up. A professional. A man who probably has given hundreds of women a massage and doesn't see anything sexual in this.

Meanwhile, I'm lying here like a Victorian widow discovering the joys of hysteria treatment.

His hands move to my arms. My forearms. My hands. He presses each palm in turn, working his thumbs in little circles near the base of my thumbs, and somehow that's worse—gentler. More intimate. Like he knows how tired I am.

His thumbs circle one last time at the base of my palm, then gently release it back onto the sheet.

I feel the absence like a gust of cold air.

There's a pause. A flicker of stillness in the music.

"Would you like more of your back done?" His voice is soft. Low. Still perfectly neutral—which only makes my body react more.

I swallow. "Yes, please."

Bloody hell. I sound so prim it is laughable.

He shifts behind me. I hear the faint rustle of fabric, and then feel the sheet slowly sliding lower. He tucks it in just above the base of my spine—just enough to give him room to work, without exposing anything I'd need therapy to recover from.

"You okay?" he checks.

"Mm-hmm," I manage, my voice doing that tight, squeaky thing it does when I'm lying through my teeth. I am not okay. I am one well-placed sigh away from spontaneous combustion.

He starts again, this time with more oil—his hands warmer, slower. Gliding from the middle of my back to the dip of my waist in long, hypnotic strokes. There's more skin contact now. More silence. More… everything.

My clit tingles.

My heart does something unhelpful in the region of *are you falling for him?* which I ignore forcefully.

Then, as his fingers pause at the band of my bra, he asks innocently "I can't work around this bit easily without getting oil on it. Do you want to unhook it?"

It's not a question with a hidden meaning. It's practical. Professional. A standard part of any massage.

But still, my brain short-circuits.

"Right. Yes. Sorry."

I reach back, awkwardly fumbling with the clasp like a hormonal teenager. It takes two tries—because of course it does—but eventually it pops open, and I lie flat again, trying not to combust.

Jasper doesn't say anything. Doesn't hesitate. He simply resumes, hands pressing and sweeping over the newly freed area—the space between my shoulder blades, the top of my spine, the place where tension knots like bad memories.

And suddenly I'm melting.

Not just relaxing—*melting*. Like everything tight and wired in me is loosening, bit by bit, under the steady rhythm of his touch. There's something quiet in it. Something careful. And that quiet starts to make me feel something very close to safe.

Which is ridiculous.

Because I'm half-naked under a towel and he's technically my landlord.

But also, he's Jasper.

And right now, Jasper is undoing me in slow, steady increments—without saying a word, without crossing a line, without needing anything from me except permission to keep going.

It's unnerving.

It's addictive.

And somewhere, in the middle of all that slow release, a realisation blooms—soft and inconvenient:

I don't just want his hands.

I want him.

Fuck. Fuck. Fuckity fuck!

17

Hark! The Herald Angels Blush

Jasper

My hands move in slow, deliberate strokes, when I sense her body finally fully relax beneath my touch. The soft glow of the candles casts a warm light across the room, and the scent of lemon in the air is soothing. I'm about to announce that we're done, to tell her she can take her time getting up, when her voice breaks the silence.

"Lower," she whispers, her tone barely audible. I pause, my hands hovering over her skin, thinking I must have misheard. But then she repeats it, her voice steady this time, leaving no room for doubt:

"Lower?" I ask, more to confirm than to question, my heart skipping a beat. She nods slightly, her blonde hair brushing against her shoulder. I take a deep breath, my fingers trembling ever so slightly as I push the sheet further down to expose the top of her bum. I start massaging, my hands gliding over the curves, my touch gentle yet firm. The room feels charged, the air thick with unspoken desire.

"Lower!" she demands with a slightly shaky voice. I should stop this because I am not convinced she is aware of what she is asking. But I don't. I can't.

I push the sheet completely off her and wait to see her reaction. She just sighs and slowly spreads her legs a tiny bit. It is a sign. An invitation. And nothing can stop me now.

As my fingers slide between her legs, I feel the dampness through her knickers, a warmth that surprises me. Miranda's breath hitches, and I pause again, unsure if I should continue. But her body language is clear—she's inviting me in. Carefully, I push the gusset of her knickers aside, my touch deliberate, as if I'm handling something fragile. Her skin is soft, her wetness undeniable, and I realise this isn't just a massage anymore. It's something more, something intimate and unspoken.

I begin an intimate massage, my fingers tracing the contours of her body, my touch slow and purposeful. Miranda lets out a soft moan, her hands gripping the edges of the table. "Jasper," she murmurs, her voice laced with desire. I don't respond with words; instead, I let my hands speak for me. My fingers dip lower, exploring, teasing, until I feel her tremble beneath me.

Her wetness coats my fingers, and I can't ignore the way my own body is reacting to her.

Before I know it, I'm inside her, my fingers sliding deep, responding to her unspoken invitation. Miranda arches her back, her head tilting back as a soft gasp escapes her lips. "Yes," she breathes, her voice a mixture of pleasure and surrender. I move slowly, my touch deliberate, my fingers fucking her with a rhythm that feels natural, as if we've done this a thousand times before. My thumb draws circles around her clit whilst my free hand massaged her shoulders.

My cock is rock hard and I am rubbing it against the edge of the massage table to get some kind of release. This is so wrong but it all feels so right.

The room is filled with the sounds of her breathing, her moans, and the soft wetness of her body responding to my fingers.

I lean closer, my lips brushing against her ear. "Is this what you wanted?" I whisper, my voice rough with desire. She nods, her hands reaching back to grip my wrists, urging me deeper.

"Yes," she says, her voice firm yet breathless. "Don't stop." And I don't. My fingers move faster, my touch more insistent, and I feel her body tense, her muscles tightening around me. Her breath comes in short gasps, and I know she's close.

"Jasper," she moans, her voice pleading, her body arching off the table. I press my lips to her shoulder, my breath hot against her skin, as I feel her climax ripple through her. Her body shakes, her wetness spilling over my fingers, and I hold her there, my touch steady, until she collapses back onto the table, her breath ragged.

I stay with her for a moment longer, my hands gentling, then easing away entirely. The shift in the room is almost physical. The moment folds in on itself—still warm, still charged, but rapidly fraying at the edges.

"I'll give you a second," I say, voice quiet. Measured. I don't look at her face. I don't dare.

Instead, I cross to the kitchen and wash my hands whilst pretending, for both our sakes, that my heartbeat isn't thudding through every joint. That my hands aren't still warm from her.

Behind me, there's the soft rustle of movement. The quiet sound of fabric against skin. The slight shuffle of her slipping back into the robe. Every small sound feels louder than it should. Or maybe that's just the silence sitting between us now.

I let out a slow breath, centring myself. I'm hard. Obviously. No amount of steady breathing's fixing that just yet. But this isn't about me. Never was. I give it space. Let it burn itself down. Quiet the part of me that's screaming to go back to the table and—

"Okay," Miranda says, her voice back—not shaky, not soft. Just... composed. Dignified, even.

I turn around slowly. She's got the robe tied neatly, her cheeks still flushed, her hair slightly mussed. She's trying for casual. Pulling it off, almost. But her eyes catch mine, and something flickers.

"Feel better?" I ask, careful not to layer the words too thick.

She nods.

There's a pause—not long, not uncomfortable. Just heavy. Weighted. Her fingers brush the edge of the robe's tie, then drop.

"I should go," I say, my voice a little rougher than intended.

She doesn't stop me. Just gives a quick nod. "Thanks again... for everything."

I grab my things slowly, methodically—the towel, the oil, the table. It feels weirdly ceremonial. Like cleaning up after something holy, only with a foldable massage table and a wildly unprofessional erection that I'm doing my best to pretend never happened.

At the door, I turn back.

She's standing where I left her, near the sofa, back straight, chin up—but her eyes are following me like she's not quite ready for me to be gone. Like part of her still hasn't come down from wherever she was.

"Miranda."

She locks eyes with me.

And I say it before I talk myself out of it.

"Would you have dinner with me?"

The silence stretches—not awkward, just... sharp. Like we've stepped onto a new line and neither of us is sure how deep the water goes.

Her brows lift slightly. "Dinner?"

"Not as a favour. Not as a thank-you. Just... dinner. With me. Because I'd really like to take you out."

She hesitates for a beat, eyes flicking to mine like she's searching for the catch. Then, softly, "I'm chaos."

I smile. "I like chaos."

That earns me the smallest laugh, real, if a little surprised. "Saturday, then," she says. "SJ's at his dad's again."

"Saturday it is."

We stand there for a moment longer, both pretending we're not still buzzing from everything that came before.

Then she smiles, properly this time. "Goodnight, Jasper."

"'Night, Miranda."

I close the door behind me. The air's colder now, but somehow, I feel warmer than I have in weeks.

18

It's Beginning to Look a Lot Like Co-parenting

Miranda

I'm standing in the middle of my bedroom, staring at a growing mountain of clothes on the bed while Thor attacks a sleeve like a thousand treats are hidden in it.

Twinklesocks surveys the chaos from a nest of scarves, tail twitching with disapproval. She looks like she's considering pressing charges.

I hold up a navy wrap dress. Classic. Elegant. Also last worn to a parent-teacher conference where I got told SJ had "too many opinions about the usefulness of Maths." I toss it aside. The pile grows.

Thor launches himself off the chest of drawers and lands belly-first in a tangle of tights. He wriggles like a ferret, pops his head out of one leg hole, and meows triumphantly.

"No one invited you to this crisis," I say, kneeling to rescue a silk top from his claws. He immediately bats at my hair. "Saboteur."

The bedroom floor is a battlefield: shoes with no partners, hangers that have staged a coup, a lone bra flung across the dresser like it surrendered early. I dig out a green blouse. Hold it up. Too shiny. Back in the pile.

I glance at the mirror.

My cheeks are bright red. My hair's doing its own thing. And somewhere in all of this, I've lost my glass of wine.

The date isn't until tomorrow. It's just dinner. But my heart's thudding like I'm due onstage and forgot to memorise my lines.

The doorbell rings.

I freeze, one hand still tangled in the navy wrap dress, the other trying to fend off Thor, who's decided my bra strap is the enemy. Twinklesocks has climbed into the laundry basket and is kneading a sequin skirt.

The bell goes again. Longer this time.

"Fuck. Sim-Sim."

I groan, dropping the dress. It slipped my mind that he's popping by to collect SJ's Arsenal kit.

Kittens scatter as I step over a jumble of cardigans, still barefoot, a bit sweaty, and looking like I lost a fight with a discount rail.

I unlock the front door and swing it open.

Sim-Sim's standing there in jeans and a soft-looking jumper, hands in his pockets, hair slightly windswept like he walked over without checking a mirror—but still somehow manages to look effortlessly put together.

"Hey," he says with a small smile.

"Come in," I reply, stepping aside. "Before the kittens try to launch themselves into traffic."

He steps in just as Twinklesocks appears as if she heard the word *escape* and is ready to commit. I nudge her back with my foot as he shuts the door behind him.

His eyes skim over me—oversized jumper, leggings, bun barely holding its shape.

"You look nice," he says.

I huff a laugh. "I look like I've been wrestling a tumble dryer."

He shrugs. "Still beautiful, though."

Something twists in my stomach—confusion, maybe. Or indigestion. Definitely not helpful.

"Give me a sec," I mutter, already halfway down the hall. Since SJ and I moved out here, my interactions with Sim-Sim have improved. I don't know if it is the distance or that I no longer spend every waking minute plotting his demise, but something has shifted. It reminds me of the time back before we got together.

SJ's room is a mess of Lego, half-folded clothes, and at least three socks that may or may not be from the same century. I unearth the Arsenal shirt from beneath a suspiciously glittery hoodie, fold it with a half-hearted pat, and head back.

When I return, Sim-Sim's standing in the middle of the living room, holding Thor like he's some kind of purring prize. The kitten's draped across his arm, eyes half-closed, vibrating with smug contentment.

"He jumped into my arms," Sim-Sim says with a soft smile. "Didn't have the heart to move him."

"Traitor," I mutter to Thor, but my voice comes out warmer than I intend.

Sim-Sim's thumb rubs just under the kitten's chin, and Thor leans into it like a cat who's suddenly forgotten he lives here.

"Here." I offer the shirt, and he reaches out with one hand to take it, careful not to dislodge the feline royalty currently using him as a mattress.

"Thanks." He glances down at the folded fabric. "Big match tomorrow. He'll be gutted if we lose."

"We can't have that," I say lightly, nodding at the shirt like it's the most important object in the room.

Silence settles between us, soft and awkward. Thor purrs like a small engine, oblivious to the tension he's nestled right in the middle of.

Sim-Sim looks down at the kitten for a long second, his fingers still gently stroking behind one tiny ear.

Then, without looking up, he says quietly, "I miss you."

My breath catches—not dramatically, not even audibly. Just enough for me to notice. To feel the words land and slide under my skin.

There's no push in his voice. No expectation. Just a simple truth dropped between us like it won't change the air—even though it already has.

"Why are you saying that?" I ask, not sharp, just... tired. I already know the answer, but I need to hear it anyway.

Sim-Sim's eyes lift to mine. "Because it's true," he says simply. "And because there have been a million times I've wished I could undo what I've done."

My arms fold tighter around my ribs.

"It's too late now," I say, quietly. Not to hurt him. Just because it is... I think.

He nods. Once. No argument. Just the softest downturn of his mouth as he looks back at Thor, whose purring somehow feels louder now, like he's trying to fill the silence.

"Yeah," he murmurs. "I know."

He gives Thor a last stroke, then carefully lowers him to the floor. The kitten lets out a small, offended chirp and pads off in search of someone more emotionally stable.

Simon moves towards the door. I scoop up Twinklesocks with one arm and nudge Thor back with my foot before he can attempt another dramatic exit.

Sim-Sim pauses with his hand on the handle. "Could we have a coffee next week? To talk about Christmas plans?"

I shift the kitten slightly in my arms. "We can do that over the phone."

He glances back at me, the corner of his mouth lifting, but his eyes still serious. "Miranda… just a coffee."

There's a beat. I hate how uncertain I feel, how some part of me still wants to keep everything perfectly compartmentalised.

But I nod. "Fine. Come over during one of my lunch breaks."

His smile softens. "Text me when you're free."

And then he's gone, the door clicking softly behind him.

Twinklesocks lets out a little squeak, clearly unimpressed by the lack of drama. Thor sprawls exhausted at my feet.

I blow out hard then look around at the quiet flat, the abandoned wine glass, and the pile of half-folded clothes in my room.

Just a coffee.

Right.

There's a pair of tights dangling from the lampshade, one kitten stuck inside a laundry basket, and I'm wearing a face mask that smells faintly of regret.

Amelia's perched on the edge of my bed, cradling a novelty mug that says *Mum Fuel* in chunky pink letters. Steam curls from the top, and she looks far too calm for someone about to launch a full-blown intervention.

"Right," she says, taking a sip, "let's talk about your moustache."

I blink at her. "Sorry—what moustache?"

She leans in slightly, eyes narrowing. "The little blond one. You can only see it when the light hits just right, but trust me, it's there."

I slap a hand over my upper lip. "Why has no one told me this before?"

Amelia shrugs, unbothered. "Because we love you and didn't want you to descend into a spiral. But you're going on a date now. A date that might involve candlelight. And proximity. So we defuzz."

"I don't want to defuzz!"

"You will when you're sitting across from him wondering if he's admiring your lip foliage instead of your witty banter."

I groan and flop backwards on the bed, dislodging a confused Twinklesocks, who had been very much enjoying my stomach as a mattress. Amelia gives the kitten a gentle nudge and sets her tea down with purpose.

"Miranda. You are stunning. You have an excellent dress, a decent pair of shoes, and a man who probably dreams in HD about you. Now sit up. Let me pluck your face."

"I feel like a prize heifer at a county fair."

Amelia grins. "A very sexy prize heifer. With great bone structure."

I'm mid-flinch as Amelia brandishes a pair of tweezers when I blurt, "Sim-Sim came over last night."

She pauses, tweezers frozen mid-air. "What, with a boombox and a tragic mixtape?"

"No," I say, rolling my eyes. "To pick up SJ's football shirt."

"Ah. The classic pretext." She tilts her head, studying me. "And?"

"And... he said he misses me."

Amelia lowers the tweezers slowly. "Well. That's not nothing."

"I told him it's too late," I mutter. "Which it is."

She nods, then sips from her tea. "Did he do the full sad-eyes routine?"

"No. It wasn't a performance. Just honest. Quiet. No pressure."

Amelia sets the mug down on the dressing table, fingers tapping once against the ceramic. "And how did that feel? Really?"

I hesitate. "Strange. Familiar. Not awful. He asked me to meet him for a coffee to discuss Christmas plans."

Her brows knit, the humour dropping from her face. "Miranda, I know it's not my business—"

"You're about to make it your business, though."

"Damn right," she says gently. "I just... I don't want you getting pulled back into something that made you feel small."

I blink. "I'm not."

"I know," she says. "But even strong people forget what the cage looked like once the door's been open a while."

That stops me.

She sighs. “Look, I’m not saying don’t have coffee. I’m not even saying don’t be civil. But you’ve built something for yourself. Stability. Space. And tonight—Jasper. That’s something new. Something that makes you light up when you don’t know you’re doing it.”

I look away, fiddling with a hairbrush.

“I’m fine,” I say eventually.

“I know you are. You always are.” She pauses, then adds quietly, “Just don’t forget who you were before the divorce. And who you’ve become since.”

Her words settle in my chest like a stone skipping once, twice—then sinking.

I don’t say anything at first. Just turn and pull her into a hug, careful of her tea. She squeezes me back without hesitation, all solid comfort and quiet strength.

“Thanks,” I murmur against her shoulder.

She pulls away a little, eyes kind. “Anytime. Though now, I do believe we’ve got more urgent matters—like the rogue fluff on your bum.”

I groan. “I swear, if you whip out that lint roller again—”

Amelia already has it in hand, brandished like a weapon. “Stand up. You’re wearing black. This is war.”

And just like that, we’re back in the fray—her crouched behind me like a determined valet, muttering about rogue cat hairs and my apparently invisible upper-lip situation, while I try not to cry-laugh into a throw pillow.

Honestly, who needs enemies when you've got a best friend like this?

19

The First Moan-el

Jasper

The dining room glows with candlelight and polished silverware. Everything here is hushed elegance—from the soft clink of glasses to the gentle murmurs of other tables—but somehow, we're making it our own. Miranda's eyes sparkle more with every sip of wine, and I swear I haven't stopped smiling since we sat down.

"...and I just froze," she says, eyes wide. "Like full statue mode. Clipboard in one hand, traumatised stare in the other. Stella's lipstick was halfway down her neck and Callum—well, let's just say his trousers were not where trousers should be."

I nearly choke on a sip of wine. "In the office?"

"In the office," she confirms grimly. "I was dropping off meeting notes. I backed out as quickly as I could."

I snort. "Please tell me you brought it up in a team meeting."

She levels me with a look. "Absolutely not. This stays between us. I mean it, Corbin… secrecy or death."

I raise a hand solemnly. "I take my oaths seriously."

She grins, taking another sip of her wine, and I let myself take her in for a moment—the way she laughs with her whole face, the curve of her cheekbone when she smirks, the slightly flustered little tug she gives the sleeve of her dress whenever she's trying not to seem flirty.

She's stunning. In that chaotic, grounded, utterly magnetic way she probably doesn't even realise.

"Tell me more about your brothers," she says, tucking a loose strand of hair behind her ear. "You've mentioned them, but I don't really know anything."

I smile, leaning back slightly. "Well, there's Geoff: oldest, photographer, moody, lives in a wool mill conversion in Highbury like he's too artistic for walls that match. He's the one who used to lock us in the airing cupboard when Mum wasn't looking."

She raises her brows. "Charming."

"Oh, completely. He once convinced me that chocolate is made from bugs. I didn't eat any for a year."

She laughs. "And the other brother?"

"Theo. Middle child. He's the nice one. Runs a coffee shop, amazing dad to Lucy, and somehow manages to look like he's just stepped out of a wholesome Netflix romcom. Which to be fair is not too far from the truth because he found the love of his life recently."

Miranda grins. "So basically, one evil genius, one cardigan-wearing saint, and you."

I raise my glass. "The well-adjusted youngest."

Miranda rests her chin lightly on her hand, eyes dancing across the candlelit table. "You don't seem like the youngest," she says. "Too... sorted."

"Is that a compliment or an accusation?"

She considers it. "Bit of both."

I chuckle, swirling the last of my wine. "And you? Only child?"

She shakes her head. "Older sister. Bossy. Took the lead in everything. Including giving me a fringe when we were nine."

"Oof. Did it involve kitchen scissors and a false sense of confidence?"

"Obviously. I looked like a startled mushroom for six months."

I grin. "I'd have liked to see that."

She gives me a look. "You'd have laughed."

"Only a little."

She leans forward slightly, eyes catching the glow of the table lamp. "You're very sure of yourself."

I shrug. "I've had practice. Plus, I'm sitting across from a woman who admitted to watching gay porn and still somehow has the upper hand."

She nearly chokes on her drink, laughing. "That was supposed to be forgotten."

"Never. Etched into my soul."

A beat passes, her laughter softening into a smile that lingers just long enough to shift something between us.

Then I glance up, catch the waiter's eye, and say, "Shall we get the bill?"

We step out into the crisp night, the cold slipping beneath collars and brushing against flushed cheeks. The car park is quiet, save for the distant hum of tyres on wet tarmac and the faint rustle of trees in the breeze.

I lead her towards the car, the gravel crunching beneath our feet. She's saying something—something about the dessert wine and how it always tastes like raisins mixed with soap—but I've lost the thread. Because suddenly, she's looking at me in that way again.

Like she's not entirely sure what's happening. But she's not stepping back either.

When we reach the car, I move to open the passenger door for her. But I don't. Not right away.

Instead, I reach up, just enough to slide my hand behind her head.

She stills and I wait for a rejection that never comes.

Her gaze flicks to mine, searching. Then she tips her chin up just a fraction and that's all the permission I need.

I lean in and kiss her.

Soft, careful. The kind of kiss you can still walk back from, if you need to. Testing the waters.

But she kisses me back. Her hands slide up my chest, fingers curling into my jacket as I step in closer, pressing her gently against the side of the car. I deepen the kiss, still slow, still measured, but with heat behind it now.

Her mouth opens beneath mine with a soft, unguarded sound. My hand's still in her hair. The other finds her waist. I want to pull her closer. I want—

I break the kiss before I lose all good sense.

We're both breathing hard. She blinks up at me, lips parted, dazed in the loveliest way.

"Hi," I murmur, because it's the only word that doesn't feel absurd.

She huffs a laugh. "Hi."

And just like that, the air changes again. Less charged. More... something else. Something promising.

I open the car door properly this time, and she slips in, eyes still on mine as she settles into the seat.

The drive back is quiet, but not awkward. There's a buzz between us now, subtle but insistent, like the last chord of a song still hanging in the air. At a red light, I shift in my seat and glance at her.

Her hand is resting on her thigh—close, inviting. I reach over, palm up, and after the briefest hesitation, she slips her hand into mine. Our fingers thread together like it's the most natural thing in the world.

She doesn't look at me, just smiles out the window, but I see it. The way her thumb brushes lightly against mine. The way she shifts a little closer in her seat.

And we stay like that, quietly connected, all the way home.

When I pull up in the drive, I kill the engine but don't move from my seat. Neither does she.

She turns to me, lips parted like she might say something but I lean in and kiss her again.

This one's slower. Less urgency, more intention. Her hand comes up to rest lightly against my chest, fingers curling into the fabric of my coat like she wants to anchor herself there.

When we part, I don't move far. Just enough to speak against her lips. "I don't want the evening to be over."

Her eyes flick to mine, warm and a little breathless. "It doesn't have to be."

My heart does a quiet, smug little somersault.

"But..." she adds, teasing now, "if we go to mine, I have to share you with Twinklesocks."

I grin. "She does love me. But let's head to mine so I can give you my full attention."

She nods, lips curving. "Lead the way."

The moment the front door clicks shut behind us, Miranda's lips are on mine, fierce and hungry. There's no preamble, no easing into it—just raw, urgent need. Her hands are already in my hair, tugging gently as she presses against me, her body warm and insistent. I wrap an arm around her waist, pulling her closer, feeling the soft curves of her frame against my chest. My fingers fumble with the zip, her skin brushing against mine, electric and alive.

"Fuck, I want this so much," she murmurs between kisses, her breath hot on my lips. Her voice is thick with desire. I don't bother responding with words; instead, I deepen the kiss, my tongue tangling with hers, tasting the sweetness of her lipstick, the hint of wine from earlier. Her hands slide down my back, nails scraping lightly over my shirt, and I shiver at the sensation.

We're moving before I even realise it, stumbling toward the bedroom, clothes becoming an afterthought. My jacket hits the floor first, followed by her dress, which pools around her ankles. She steps out of it gracefully, her underwear a delicate lace that contrasts with the wildness of the moment. I pause for a fraction of a second, taking in the sight of her—her blonde hair tousled, her cheeks pink, her eyes sparkling with want. She's breathtaking, and I'm acutely aware of how lucky I am to have her here, in my arms, in my house.

"Come on," she whispers, tugging at my shirt, and I let her pull it over my head, tossing it aside without a second thought. Her fingers trace the muscles of my chest, and I feel a surge of pride at her touch, at the way her gaze lingers on me.

We're kissing again as we reach the bedroom, the bed a welcome sight. I push her gently backward until she's lying on the mattress, her hair fanning out against the pillows. I follow her down, my weight careful not to crush her, but I can't resist the urge to hover above her, to feel the power of the moment. Her legs wrap around my waist, pulling me closer, and I groan into her mouth, my hands roaming over her body, mapping every curve, every dip.

"Jasper," she sighs, her voice a plea, and I know exactly what she wants. I trail kisses down her neck, her collarbone, my lips brushing against the lace of her bra. She arches her back, pressing herself into me, and I take my time, teasing her, my fingers working the clasp of her bra until it gives way. I pull it off slowly, tossing it aside, and her breasts are revealed, full and soft, her nipples already tight with anticipation.

"Someone is enjoying this," I growl.

I take one in my mouth, sucking gently, and she gasps, her hands tangling in my hair. "Fuck, Jasper," she moans, her voice shaking, and I smile against her skin, the vibration sending a shiver through her. I switch to the other breast, lavishing it with the same attention, my hands moving down her body, over her stomach, her hips. She's squirming beneath me, her legs tightening around me, and I can feel her heat through the thin fabric of her knickers.

"Tell me what you want," I murmur, my lips brushing against hers, my breath hot and heavy.

"You," she replies without hesitation. "I want you. Now."

Her words send a jolt of desire through me, and I move quickly, pulling her knickers off in one swift motion.

"Look how wet you are for me," I groan at the sight, at the scent of her, musky and sweet. I kiss my way down her body, my lips trailing over her stomach, her thighs, until I'm kneeling between her legs, her most intimate place inches from my face.

"Jasper," she whispers, her voice trembling, and I look up at her, meeting her gaze. There's a vulnerability in her eyes, a trust that makes my heart swell. I press a gentle kiss to her inner thigh, then another, moving closer, my breath ghosting over her sensitive skin. She's tense, anticipating my touch, and I take my time, teasing her, my tongue flicking lightly over her clit before I finally part her folds, tasting her, savouring her.

She cries out, her hands gripping the duvet, her body arching off the bed. I hum against her, the vibration sending her over the edge, her walls clenching around my tongue as she comes, her voice a symphony of pleasure. I stay with her, lapping at her gently, until she's trembling, spent, her breath coming in ragged gasps.

"Your turn," she says, her voice hoarse, and I chuckle, climbing back up her body, my lips brushing against hers.

"Not today, Princess, otherwise this will all be over way to quick." I'm hard, so hard, my cock aching for her. I reach for the drawer beside the bed, pulling out a condom. She takes it from me, her fingers nimble as she rolls it on, her touch sending sparks of anticipation through me.

I position myself at her entrance, teasing her, my tip pressing against her, and she rocks her hips, urging me closer. "Now," she demands, and I thrust into her, slow and deep, filling her completely. She gasps, her nails digging into my shoulders, and I hold myself there for a moment, savouring the tightness of her, the warmth of her body enveloping my cock.

"Move," she whispers, and I do, pulling out slowly before pushing back in, setting a steady rhythm. She meets my thrusts, her hips rising to greet me, her breath coming in short, sharp gasps. I'm lost in the sensation, in the way she feels around me, in the way her body moves with mine, in perfect harmony. I moan deeply whenever I push into her, I can't help it, it feels that good.

"Fuck me harder," she pleads, and I oblige, my movements becoming more urgent, more desperate. The bed creaks beneath us, the headboard knocking against the wall, but neither of us cares. We're consumed by the moment, by the raw, primal need that's taken over. Her fingers dig into my back, her legs wrapped tightly around my waist, and I can feel her walls fluttering around me.

"Come with me," I call out, my voice rough, and she nods, her eyes locked on mine. I thrust into her one last time, deep and hard, and she cries out, her body shaking as she comes, her release triggering my own. I spill into the condom, my cock pulsing, my breath ragged as I collapse on top of her, shifting my weight careful not to crush her.

We lie there for a moment, our hearts pounding, our breaths slowly syncing. I pull out gently, disposing of the condom, before settling beside her, pulling her into my arms. She rests her head on my chest, her fingers tracing patterns on my skin, and I kiss the top of her head.

The fire eases into a steady warmth, wrapping around me as surely as she does. It isn't frightening, not really. It's exhilarating, the kind of pull I've never wanted to resist. I'm falling for her, and it feels like the most natural thing in the world.

20

Sleigh My Name

Miranda

I wake to warmth. Not the sort that comes from duvets or central heating, but the kind that comes from being wrapped entirely in someone else.

Jasper's arm is heavy across my waist. His chest is pressed to my back. One of his legs has somehow managed to trap both of mine. I'm essentially burritoed in six-foot-something of sleepy man, and I'm not mad about it.

The room smells like him—clean, warm, something faintly woody—and there's a quiet hum of morning outside, car noises softened by expensive double glazing. The world is already turning, though it's still dim beyond the windows, the kind of cold, grey light that says November's not even pretending to try.

I hold my breath as I slide one arm free and begin the delicate operation of unspooling myself from his limbs.

I almost make it.

One foot hits the floor, then the other—

And then a groggy voice rumbles behind me.

"Oi."

A hand loops around my waist and I'm pulled back into bed like a very confused mermaid being netted by a fisherman.

"Jasper," I say, laughing despite myself.

"Nope," he mumbles, nuzzling into my neck. "You can't leave. Hostage rules."

"I have to feed the kittens."

"They'll survive."

"Twinklesocks will eat the curtains."

He groans dramatically and flips onto his back, dragging me with him until I'm sprawled half across his chest. His eyes are still closed, but his mouth finds mine easily, kissing me deep and slow and with enough heat to make me question every responsible decision I've ever made.

"Let me go," I whisper against his lips, "and I promise to return. Bearing pastries."

One eye cracks open. "You swear?"

"On the life of my fluffy bathrobe."

He releases me with a theatrical sigh, running a hand through his chaos of morning hair.

"Fine," he says. "But I'm timing you. Take the keys from the bowl next to the front door."

I slip on my dress and pause in the doorway, stealing one last look at him... tousled and naked, duvet low on his hips, eyes heavy with sleep and something softer.

I try not to melt. I really do.

But it's hard when he looks at me like that, all rumpled and drowsy and devastating.

Still, I manage to peel myself away and make the quick dash next door. Twinklesocks is at the cat gate waiting like she's filed a formal complaint, and Thor lets out a long, mournful meow as if I've been gone a week and not just one night.

"Alright, alright," I mutter, flicking on the kitchen light and heading straight for the food cupboard. "I'm a monster. A terrible, neglectful parent."

They forgive me the second the bowls hit the floor. Naturally.

While they devour their breakfast like starving Dickensian orphans, I get changed into some comfortable clothes, slap together some toast, make two strong mugs of tea, and try not to overthink the fact that I'm carrying breakfast for a man I definitely didn't plan to sleep with—and am now about to crawl back into bed with.

When I return, Jasper is, unsurprisingly, asleep again. Sprawled across the bed like a man who knows he has nowhere to be and isn't sorry about it. One arm flung above his head, the other resting on his chest. A bit of duvet, a lot of bare skin. And hair that looks like it's been in negotiations with a pillow for eight hours straight.

I set the tray down, slip onto the bed, and kiss him softly.

He stirs with a groan and a crooked smile. “Mmm. That’s a very good way to wake up.”

“I come bearing toast,” I say, brushing a kiss to his jaw.

“You might actually be perfect.”

“Don’t ruin it. Eat before it gets cold.”

He tugs me gently until I’m sitting next to him, one arm wrapping around my waist as I settle in. We share the toast between sips of tea, warm limbs tangled, crumbs everywhere, and not a single care given.

Then, somewhere between the last bite and the next kiss, he murmurs against my cheek, “Spend the day with me.”

I pull back just enough to see his face. “The whole day?”

He nods, thumb brushing along the hem of my T-shirt. “SJ’s not back till tomorrow, right?”

“Nope.”

“Then stay. We’ll do whatever you like. Go for a walk. Watch a terrible film. Eat more toast. Or not leave this bed at all. I’m flexible.”

I snort. “Clearly.”

But something in his tone is tender. Hopeful. And it sinks in—the idea that maybe this doesn’t have to be just one night. That maybe this could stretch into something with edges and shape and softness.

“Alright,” I say, voice light. “I’m all yours.”

“Good,” he says, pulling me closer. “Because I was going to bribe you with the last bite of my toast if necessary.”

I'm sprawled across the bed as Jasper's hands move lazily over my back. The room is bathed in the warm glow of late afternoon sunlight, filtering through the curtains and casting a golden hue over everything. We've spent the entire day here, in this cocoon of comfort, talking, laughing, and simply enjoying each other's company. It's been a while since I've felt this at ease with someone, and I can't help but marvel at the deep sense of connection with Jasper.

"How about another massage?" I murmur, my voice soft and laced with a hint of invitation. His hands pause for a moment, and I feel his gaze on me before he nods, his fingers resuming their slow, rhythmic strokes.

"Of course," he replies, his deep, soothing voice sending a shiver down my spine. "Anything for you, Miranda."

I close my eyes, letting the warmth of his touch seep into my muscles. Jasper's hands are strong yet gentle, his movements deliberate and practiced. He starts at my shoulders, kneading the tension away with firm pressure, his thumbs digging into the knots that have formed from months of stress. I let out a soft sigh, my body relaxing into the mattress as he works his way down my spine.

His hands glide lower, tracing the curve of my waist before moving to my hips. I feel his fingers press into the soft flesh, his touch firm but tender. There's something intimate about this, something that goes beyond the physical. It's as if he's not just massaging my body but also soothing my soul.

"Turn over," he says softly, his voice a low rumble that sends a flutter through my chest. I do as he asks, rolling onto my back and propping myself up on my elbows. Jasper's eyes meet mine, his gaze intense and filled with a warmth that makes my heart skip a beat. He's handsome, with his dark hair and strong features, but it's the kindness in his eyes that truly captivates me.

He begins again, his hands moving to my shoulders and then down my arms, his touch light and teasing. I feel a tingle run through me as his fingers brush over my skin, his movements slow and deliberate. There's something different about this massage, something more charged, more intimate. I can feel the air between us thicken, the tension building in a way that's both exhilarating and nerve-wracking.

"Jasper," I breathe, my voice barely above a whisper. His hands pause, and he looks at me, his expression unreadable.

"What is it?" he asks, his voice gentle.

I bite my lip, unsure how to put my thoughts into words. "This feels... different," I admit, my cheeks flushing as I meet his gaze. He smiles, a slow, knowing curve of his lips, and my heart races.

"Does it?" he asks, his tone playful. His hands move again, this time to my thighs, his fingers tracing the curve of my legs with a deliberate slowness that makes my breath catch. I feel a warmth spread through me and a heat that pools low in my belly.

"Oh my," I say with a shaky voice. He leans closer, his breath ghosting over my skin as he speaks.

"Do you want me to stop?" he asks, his voice low and husky.

I shake my head, my eyes fluttering closed as his hands continue their slow, teasing exploration.

His hands move higher, his fingers skimming the hem of my loose shirt before slipping underneath. I shiver as his touch meets my bare skin, his palms warm against my stomach. He takes his time, his movements unhurried as he traces the contours of my body, his touch both gentle and firm.

I feel my breath quicken, my body responding to his fingers in a way that's both familiar and entirely new. There's a hunger building inside me, a need that's been simmering just beneath the surface all day. Jasper's hands seem to know exactly where to go, his fingers mapping the sensitive spots that make me arch into his touch.

"You're ruining me," he murmurs, his lips brushing against my collarbone. I close my eyes, letting the words wash over me.

His hands move higher, cupping my breasts with a tenderness that makes my heart ache. I feel his thumbs brush over my nipples, and I breathe out sharply, my body tightening as pleasure spikes through me. He takes his time, teasing and edging me, his touch deliberate and unhurried.

"Oh fuck," I moan, my voice thick with need. "Please."

He smiles against my skin, his lips trailing down my chest. "Patience," he whispers, his breath hot against me. "I want to take my time with you."

I nod, though I'm not sure I have the strength to form words. His hands continue their slow exploration, his fingers tracing patterns on my skin that leave me trembling. I feel the tension building, a coil of pleasure tightening inside me, and I know I'm on the edge of something incredible.

But Jasper doesn't let me go over. He pulls back, his hands moving to my hips as he holds me in place. I whimper in frustration, my body arching toward him, desperate for more.

"Not yet," he says, his voice firm yet gentle. "I want to savour this."

I open my eyes, meeting his gaze as he leans back on his heels. He's watching me, his expression intense and filled with a desire that mirrors my own. I feel a flush creep up my cheeks, but I don't look away. There's something powerful in this moment, something raw and honest.

"What do you want, Princess?" he asks, his voice low and steady.

I take a deep breath, my heart pounding in my chest. "You," I reply, my voice steady despite the turmoil inside me. "I want you."

He smiles, a slow, satisfied curve of his lips. "Then take me," he says, his voice a challenge.

I hesitate for a moment, my mind racing with the possibilities. But as our lips meet, as his hands move to my body with a newfound urgency, I realise that this is just the beginning. The possibilities stretch out before us, endless and tantalising. And I can't wait to see where they lead.

21

I Wish It Could Be Chaos Every Day

Jasper

I'm lying on my back, shifting Miranda so she is straddling me, her blonde hair cascading over her shoulders like liquid gold. Her eyes, a deep shade of blue, lock onto mine as she lowers herself onto me, her lips curling into a mischievous smile.

"You're so fucking tight, Miranda," I whisper, my voice rough with desire. Her walls grip me like a vice, her warmth enveloping me in a way that makes my breath catch.

She moans softly, her head tilting back as she begins to move, her hips rolling in a slow, deliberate rhythm. I can feel every inch of her, her body moving in perfect harmony with mine.

It's intoxicating, the way she takes control, yet still surrenders to the moment.

"That's it, take what you need, Princess," I growl, my hands gripping her hips, pulling her closer with each thrust. Her skin is soft beneath my palms, her body responding to my touch like it was made for me. She's not just tight—she's perfect. Every movement, every sound she makes, sends a jolt of pleasure straight to my cock. I can't help but groan, my voice deepening as I lose myself in the sensation.

"Fuck, you feel incredible," I mutter, my breath quickening as she arches her back, her breasts rising and falling with her rapid breaths. Her nipples are hard, her skin flushed, and I can't resist the urge to lean up and capture one in my mouth, sucking gently as she gasps, her hands tangling in my hair.

"Don't stop," I hiss against her skin, "keep moving for me."

Miranda's moans grow louder, her movements more urgent. Her nails dig into my shoulders, her body trembling as she rides me harder, her breath coming in short, sharp bursts. I can feel her tightening around me, her muscles clenching in a way that makes my head spin.

"I'm gonna come, Miranda," I warn, my voice breaking as I thrust up to meet her, our bodies colliding in a rhythm that's both frantic and deliberate. "You make me lose control."

Her eyes widen, her lips parting in a silent cry as she nods, her body responding to my words like they're a command.

"Fuck, you're amazing," I moan, my voice hoarse as I grip her hips tighter, my thrusts becoming more desperate. She's everything I didn't know I needed, her presence filling a void I hadn't even realized existed.

The little sounds of pleasure she makes are music to my ears, and I never want her to stop making them.

As I feel my climax building, I pull her down, our lips crashing together in a kiss that's both hungry and tender. Her taste is sweet, her tongue tangling with mine as I roll us over, pinning her beneath me. She wraps her legs around my waist, her heels digging into my back as I drive my cock into her, the angle hitting a spot that makes her cry out, her body arching off the bed.

"Jasper," she pants, her voice breathless as she tightens around me again, her nails scratching down my back. "Don't stop, please." Her words are like fuel, pushing me closer to the edge. I'm teetering, my control slipping away as I thrust harder, faster, my breath coming in ragged gasps.

"Fuck, Miranda," I groan, my voice breaking as I feel her trembling beneath me, her body on the brink. "Come with me, Princess. Let go." Her eyes flutter closed, her lips parting in a silent scream as she shatters around me, her walls milking me in a way that sends me over the edge.

I bury my face in her neck, my body shaking as I spill into the condom, my moans muffled against her skin. Her hands clutch at my back, her body convulsing as she rides out her orgasm, her breath hot against my ear.

For a moment, the world narrows to just this—the feel of her, the sound of her, the scent of her. This right here is as close to perfect as I think anything can ever feel.

Callum looks up the second I walk into the pub, eyebrows raised before I've even reached the table.

"Alright," he says slowly. "You've got a look."

"A look," I repeat, dropping into the seat opposite and taking one of the waiting pints.

He nods. "Yeah. One of *those* looks. Something's happened."

I stare into my drink. I came here for a reason. I need to talk to someone—and it can't be my brothers.

"I spent the whole weekend with Miranda."

His eyes widen, then narrow. "The weekend... as in—"

I glance at him. "All weekend... in my bed."

"Well bloody hell," he says after a short, shocked pause, leaning back. "That's... quick."

"It didn't feel quick," I say. "It felt like exactly where I was supposed to be."

He doesn't grin. Doesn't mock. Just watches me for a second, then gives a slow nod.

"So it's a thing now? You and her?"

"I don't know," I admit. "But it's something. And it's not casual. At least, not for me." My heart starts racing at the thought that she could think this is only something casual.

"I figured," he says, lifting his glass. "You've been looking at her like she's made of stars for weeks."

I huff a quiet laugh and clink his glass. "That obvious?"

"Painfully."

I drain almost half of my pint in one go.

"I know it's complicated," I say, quieter now. "I know she's got history and a child and it's probably mad. But I like her. A lot."

Callum shrugs. "Then go with it. Don't overthink it. You'll know soon enough if it's something worth holding onto."

I nod, but a tiny knot still sits in my chest. Because I already know it is worth everything. The only question now is whether she feels the same.

I swirl what's left of my pint. "What are you doing for Christmas, then?"

Callum perks up slightly. "Lake District. Taking Stella up for a few days. She's got this romantic thing about snowy hills and roaring fires and overpriced shepherd's pie."

"Very civilised."

"It will be if we don't argue over whose turn it is to control the heating." He grins. "We're back on Boxing Day though. Stella's daughter is coming over with her boyfriend."

"I can't believe you're basically stepdad to someone who's what, fifteen years younger than you?" I say, half-laughing.

Callum shrugs, like it's not the first time he's heard it. "I'm not her stepdad," he says, then adds with a small smile, "... yet."

"Oh, have you set a date?" When Callum got down on one knee at Halloween, it caught everyone off guard. After all, they hadn't been together very long.

"No, but we're looking at a few venues up there." He runs a hand through his hair. "We want to give ourselves a bit of time. I know the engagement was quick, but venues book up early, so there's no harm in reserving one for about a year from now."

I laugh, shaking my head. "And here I thought I was the one moving fast."

"You are," he says, smiling. "But I should thank you because your chaos makes mine look positively textbook."

I raise my glass. "To the women that make us do things we thought we'd never do."

He clinks his against mine, then says, "Exactly. To chaos?"

22

I'll Be In Cornwall for Christmas… Maybe

Miranda

The bell above the door gives its usual polite jingle as I step into the village coffee shop, the blast of warmth and the smell of cinnamon sugar hitting me square in the face. For a moment, it's almost comforting. Almost.

Then I spot him.

Sim-Sim is already at a corner table by the window, two mugs steaming gently in front of him. He sees me and smiles, and for a fleeting second, his face softens in that way it always used to back when we started dating—like the world could tilt off its axis and he'd still be there, steady, looking at me like I hung the bloody moon.

It knocks me slightly off balance.

I tighten my grip on the strap of my handbag and walk over, pretending I don't notice *the* look. The one that says *I miss this. I miss you.*

"Hi," I say, sliding into the seat opposite.

He gestures to the mug in front of me. "Flat white. Still how you take it?"

I nod. "Thanks."

There's a small pause. Not awkward, exactly, just filled with all the things neither of us is ready to say.

So I cut through it. Businesslike. Friendly. Firm.

"I thought we could use this time to talk about what we're getting SJ for Christmas."

Sim-Sim nods, wrapping his hands around the mug like it might steady something inside him. "Just tell me what you're not getting from his list," he says lightly. "I'll cover the rest."

"Right," I say, flipping open the notes app on my phone. "So far, I've bought the Minecraft Lego, the Horrible Histories annual, and the astronaut pyjamas. I vetoed the drone, the Lego Death Star, and the inflatable kayak. Oh, and I am also getting him a skateboard."

He chuckles. "I'll take it from there, then. Drone's a maybe. No promises on the kayak."

I arch a brow. "You buy him a kayak and you are the one that is taking him every weekend."

He grins, but there's a flicker of something behind it, nervous energy, maybe. He shifts in his seat, then says, "Listen. There's something else."

I knew there would be.

He doesn't meet my eyes when he says, "I wanted to talk about Christmas Day."

I set my phone down slowly. "Okay."

"I'd like to take SJ to Cornwall," he says. "To Mum and Dad's. Like we always used to. They've already made plans. Big family thing. And we've got tickets for the Boxing Day match in Plymouth, so it'd mean being away from the 23rd to the 27th."

My mouth opens.

Closes.

Before I can find words, any words, he lifts a hand gently, like he's anticipating the protest. "Or... you could come too."

The words drop into the space between us with all the ease of a brick in a birdbath.

"You want me to come to Cornwall," I repeat slowly.

Sim-Sim nods, hopeful. "There's plenty of room at my parents'. You could have one of the guest rooms. It'd just be... nice, you know? For SJ. To have both of us there. Like old times."

His eyes flick up to meet mine, cautious but warm. "And I wouldn't mind spending a bit of time with you either."

I see it coming—the shift in his posture, the softening in his voice, the almost inevitable *I miss you* hanging just behind his eyes.

I panic.

"I'm seeing someone," I blurt.

It comes out too loud. Too fast. Like a confession and a fire alarm all rolled into one.

Sim-Sim freezes. Not dramatically—just a blink, a pause, a breath that doesn't quite go anywhere.

"Oh," he says eventually. No judgement. No anger. Just... surprise.

I glance down at my mug, my fingers suddenly very interested in the shade of my coffee. "It's new. Casual. But—yeah."

Silence stretches again, awkward and heavy, like an overstuffed coat you can't quite shrug off.

"Right," he says, finally. "Okay."

I glance up.

He's trying to smile. It almost works.

"You can still come," he says after a moment. "Just as SJ's mum. Nothing else."

I shrug, not because I don't care, but because I genuinely don't know. There's a weight in my chest I hadn't noticed until just now. "I'll think about it."

"Okay," he says gently. "Let me know."

I nod and go to sip my coffee, except it's already gone lukewarm. I set the mug down instead.

"I'm not seeing anyone, by the way," he adds casually

My head lifts.

He's not looking at me when he says it, just watching his fingers trace the rim of his cup. Like it's not a big deal. Like it's not a message.

I nod again. I have no idea why. My stomach is doing a sort of slow, confused churn. I shouldn't feel anything about this. I really shouldn't. So why do I?

"Who is it?"

"What?"

"The guy you're seeing."

"Oh." I hesitate, fingers tightening around the handle of my mug. "His name's Jasper. He's—he's from the village."

"Jasper." Sim-Sim looks up. "Your landlord?"

I blink. "How do you know he's my landlord?"

He shrugs. "SJ talks about him all the time. 'Jasper helped with the kittens.' 'Jasper fixed the pipes.' 'Jasper's teaching me how to tell if a defender's playing for offsite.'" He gives a small laugh that doesn't quite land. "I thought he was just being neighbourly."

I don't know what to say to that. I just sit there, brain humming, unsure what any of this means or should mean.

It's all tangled. Not in a dramatic, soap-opera way. Just in a real-life, very-human, why-is-this-so-complicated way.

Back at the office, I stare at the same email for the fourth time and still have no idea what it says. I click into the calendar. Then out of it. Then hover over the to-do list like it might sprout an escape tunnel.

Spoiler: it doesn't.

I've spent the entire afternoon somewhere between distracted and catatonic, and I know exactly why.

Because until that coffee with Sim-Sim, I'd been floating on cloud seven. Not nine. That would be overkill. Seven feels right. Just high enough to feel giddy, low enough that I could still function. Just.

Every evening this week, after SJ was asleep and the kittens were vaguely settled (read: passed out from whatever chaos they'd conjured during the day), Jasper would sneak in like some sort of stealthy book boyfriend. We'd curl up on my bed, sometimes talking, sometimes kissing, sometimes just lying there breathing the same air like it was enough.

And of course he would dish out the most explosive orgasms almost every night. No lawnmower-like vibrator can ever compare to this.

He'd sneak out around five every morning, tucking the duvet back around me like a crime scene he was trying not to disturb. The cats, traitorous little furballs, had quickly learned this meant early breakfast, and now begin their campaign of meowing sabotage at 4:57 sharp.

But this afternoon?

This afternoon, all that fuzz and warmth has been replaced by a headache the shape of Sim-Sim's "I'm not seeing anyone" and a very pointed memory of him watching me like I was still his to miss.

I hit the button before I can talk myself out of it. "Okay, I'm spiralling. This needs a group discussion," I mumble to myself.

Within seconds, the screen fills: Lizzie in her kitchen with a glass of wine, Fi bundled in a hoodie, Amelia adjusting her headset, and Bri propped up in bed with Zucca's tail flicking across the camera.

Lizzie squints. "Oh boy. What now?"

I groan. "I just had coffee with Sim-Sim."

Fi leans so close to the camera I can see every eyelash. "On purpose?"

"It was for SJ," I say quickly. "Christmas logistics. All very above board. Until it wasn't."

Amelia raises an eyebrow. "Define 'wasn't.'"

I take a breath. "He invited me to Cornwall. For Christmas. With him. And his parents."

Bri actually drops her phone; the cat bolts. "That's... quite a pivot from logistics."

"Apparently, SJ would love both his parents there," I explain. "I'd get my own guest room. It was all packaged as very reasonable."

Fi throws her hands in the air. "That is not reasonable. That's emotional sleight of hand in a Fair Isle jumper."

"Fi," Amelia warns, though she's smirking.

I rub my eyes. "He also said he'd enjoy hanging out with me. Not in a creepy way. Just... calm. Honest. Like he meant it."

Everyone goes quiet. The little boxes on my screen are frozen, thoughtful.

Finally, Lizzie tilts her head. "Do you... want to go?"

"I don't know. That's the problem. I shouldn't even be this shaken. I'm happy. I really am."

Amelia's voice softens. "We know. But happy doesn't erase history. Especially not when it's wrapped up in your whole childhood."

"I told him I'm seeing someone," I confess. "It just... slipped out."

Fi jabs her finger at the screen. "Which is true, yeah?"

"Yes. Sort of. It's early. Not official. But Jasper makes me feel like... maybe life doesn't have to be something I brace for." Saying it out loud knots my throat.

"That sounds like a good thing," Bri says, now stroking Zucca who's returned in triumph.

Lizzie nods. "It does. But it's also fine if you're still unravelling the rest. No one's expecting you to have a five-year plan."

"And whatever you decide—Cornwall or not, Jasper or not—we're here," Amelia adds. "Promise."

I blink fast, smile watery. "I just don't know what I feel. About anything."

"That's allowed," Fi says. "You've got time."

"And for what it's worth," Lizzie adds, "no one said you have to decide who you're building a life with this week."

I laugh weakly. "Tell that to my nervous system."

Amelia leans toward the camera, deadpan. "I'd tell it to your ex if I could. But alas, we must all behave."

"For now," I mutter, and all four screens light up with laughter.

We leave it at that. I look down at my phone, then out the window where the early evening light is already folding in on itself. I'm happy.

I think I'm happy.

So why is everything so tangled?

23

Frosty the Standoff

Miranda

The village green looks like a snow globe someone forgot to shake—lights twinkling in every tree, fake snow sticking in suspicious clumps to the tinsel-strangled stalls, and a brass band doing its best to keep 'Hark! The Herald' from falling apart at the seams.

SJ is practically vibrating beside me in that way only children can manage without spontaneously combusting. He's had that look ever since we finished decorating our tree this morning. Admittedly, it was more of a battle than a tradition, thanks to Twinklesocks and Thor, who remain firmly convinced that baubles exist purely for their personal amusement. By the end of it, SJ was laughing so hard he nearly toppled into the tree, while I was rescuing ornaments mid-air like some sort of festive goalkeeper.

"Can I have a sausage?" SJ asks, eyes wide, already halfway turned toward the food stalls. "With ketchup? And onions?"

I open my mouth to say yes but Jasper beats me to it.

"Sausage mission accepted," he says, with a little salute that makes SJ beam.

"Hang on, I've got ten quid here somewhere," I say automatically, fishing in my bag.

He just smiles, that calm, maddening smile. "I've got it."

"Jasper—"

"Let me do something vaguely gallant," he murmurs, nudging my hand away with the gentlest of gestures. "One festive meat product won't break me."

I roll my eyes, but the corner of my mouth tugs upward. "Fine. But next round's on me."

"Sure." And then he's turning to Callum and Stella—who are bickering cheerfully over whether mulled wine counts as one of their five-a-day—and taking their order too.

SJ grabs Jasper's sleeve. "I'll help."

"Excellent," Jasper says solemnly. "I need a ketchup consultant."

The two of them weave through the crowd toward the sausage stall, SJ walking like he's on a covert operation and Jasper trailing behind like the world's most affable bodyguard.

I watch them go, arms crossed mostly for warmth. Jasper doesn't look back—which is probably for the best. If he did, he'd see the stupid smile I can't seem to suppress.

It's just a few dates. Amazing kisses. A warm bed and too much texting.

But somehow, he already feels... woven in. He just fits like he has always been part of my life.

"Want some wine?" Stella asks beside me, nudging her paper cup my way.

"God, yes."

She hands it over just as I catch sight of SJ holding a wad of napkins like they're state secrets, and Jasper pointing solemnly at the array of condiments like he's walking him through military strategy.

The lights reflect off Jasper's hair, that too-long bit at the front curling just enough to make me want to run my fingers through it. Which, of course, I can't.

Not here.

Not yet.

I take a sip of mulled wine, savour the warmth, and watch them laughing in the queue—my son and the man I'm trying very hard not to fall for—and wonder, not for the first time, how I ever thought I had this whole thing under control.

Stella wanders off to inspect the handmade wreaths, leaving me and Callum awkwardly babysitting our mulled wine near the bandstand.

Across the green, I can see SJ bouncing excitedly at Jasper's side, holding a sausage that's about half the length of his arm. Jasper is pretending to listen with solemn intensity, though I'm fairly sure SJ's just explained the entire Premier League table using condiments.

I take a sip of wine, trying not to smile like an idiot.

Callum follows my gaze, then glances back at me.

"I've known Jasper for years," he says, tone easy, "but I've never seen him like this."

My pulse skips. I force a small, confused-sounding laugh. "Like what?"

Callum raises an eyebrow, clearly not fooled. "Oh, come on."

I attempt another sip of wine but find my cup suspiciously empty. Callum clinks his own against mine, smirking.

"Whatever's going on," he says, "good on you both."

I barely register Callum's toast before a hand finds the small of my back.

Not a casual brush. A familiar touch.

I turn.

Sim-Sim's smile is easy, like we've just bumped into each other at the school gates. His coat's sharp, scarf knotted neatly. Effortless, like always. My spine straightens before I can stop it.

"What... are you doing here?" I blurt out.

He jerks his chin toward the field. "SJ invited me. Said I'd miss out if I didn't come. Apparently, there are sausages involved."

I glance automatically toward the food stands, where SJ is mid-order, gesturing wildly with a napkin while Jasper chats to the guy manning the grill.

I look back at Sim-Sim. "Right. That makes sense."

His hands slide into his pockets. He shifts his weight like he's bracing for something, or maybe trying not to say it.

"I wasn't trying to ambush you," he adds. "Didn't think it'd be a big deal."

My eyebrows lift.

He sees it. Offers a slight wince. "Okay. Maybe a small deal."

A beat of silence.

Then, because apparently I enjoy leaning into social landmines, I step sideways and gesture between them.

"Sim-Sim," I say, "this is Callum, my boss, and Stella, his PA-slash-girlfriend." I hesitate a beat, then sigh. "Sim-Sim, I mean, Simon is... SJ's dad."

There's a round of polite nods. Callum's jaw is tight, his expression cool but not impolite. Stella's trying to smile without looking too nosy, which, frankly, is an impossible task when I've just introduced my ex whilst the man she knows I'm dating is a few feet away.

Sim-Sim, to his credit, doesn't flinch. "Pleasure," he says easily.

And then, just in time to throw petrol on the awkward fire, SJ comes charging back, Jasper close behind.

"Dad!" he yells, launching himself into Sim-Sim's side.

Jasper arrives a second later, balancing an impressive number of sausage buns. SJ points at one with glee. "Mum, look how big Jasper's sausage is!"

Callum makes a strangled sound. Stella doubles over, mulled wine sloshing perilously close to the rim.

"Right," I mutter, pinching the bridge of my nose.

Jasper, entirely unfazed, casts a glance at Sim-Sim, then shifts the sausage tray to one hand and extends the other. "Jasper Corbin."

Sim-Sim adjusts his posture, gives a smile with just the right amount of charm, and accepts the handshake. "Simon Gordon. Good to finally meet you."

Their handshake is brief but loaded. The sort of handshake that says, *I will keep my eyes on you.*

Jasper nods, eyes cool. "Didn't know you'd be joining us."

"SJ invited me. Didn't want to miss the fun," Sim-Sim says easily.

"Oh, I thought you lived in London?" Jasper asks, tone light.

"Still do," Sim-Sim replies. "But you make time for the important things."

Jasper smiles. "True. Some things are worth making the effort for."

"Exactly." Sim-Sim glances at me, then back at Jasper. "Especially this time of year."

"Oh, the fair's brilliant," Jasper agrees, somehow managing to not break eye contact. "Magic's everywhere if you know where to look."

I resist the urge to throw myself into the mulled wine vat.

Sim-Sim tilts his head slightly. "Didn't know landlords hung out with their tenants. Seems... above and beyond."

Jasper's smile doesn't falter. "The satisfaction of my tenant is my number one priority. And that includes activities other than just fixing her pipes."

There is another snort from Callum who is clearing enjoying the ludicrous exchange.

"How... considered," Sim-Sim says. "But she can always call me as well if something needs fixing."

"No need, I' m right next door," Jasper replies, calm as anything. "That's the advantage when you rent in a small village."

The tension is wrapped in velvet, but it's definitely there. Like a duel with pistols and somehow, I guess I'm the prize. I scoff down my sausage to stop me from saying anything.

"I always figured it's better to own," Sim-Sim adds. "Fewer strings."

Jasper's brow lifts just slightly. "Depends what you're attached to." Jasper turns to me suddenly, his voice light. "Oh—you've got some ketchup."

Before I can react, he cups my chin with a gentleness and wipes the smudge from the corner of my mouth with his thumb. Then, eyes twinkling, he pulls back and sucks the ketchup of his finger.

"Rescue mission successful," he says, all mock-serious. "Your dignity is restored."

I try very hard not to combust on the spot.

SJ is busy inspecting the sausage-to-bun ratio on his own plate. But Sim-Sim isn't. His gaze latches onto Jasper's hand like it personally offended him. He steps back, just slightly, enough to say *Noted* without a word.

Jasper doesn't gloat. But the corner of his mouth tilts up with the quiet smugness of a man who knows *exactly* what he's doing.

Callum raises his cup in salute. "If either of you starts peeing a circle round Miranda, I'm out."

Stella chokes on her drink. Sim-Sim's jaw tenses.

I make a noise somewhere between a laugh and a groan. "Can we *not* make me the prize in a festive pissing contest?"

Callum shrugs. "Bit late for that, love."

SJ's dragging his feet now, glow stick limp in one hand, scarf falling off the back of his coat. He yawns without even trying to hide it.

The three of us walk in silence.

Sim-Sim's beside me. He hasn't said a word since we left the green. He is just walking in this steady pace he's always had. Calm. Familiar. Hands in pockets. Exactly how he's walked me home a hundred times before.

I'd told Jasper not to walk with us—said it lightly, like it didn't mean anything. "Stay with Callum and Stella. Pop by later."

He just nodded.

But there was a pause. And that look. Not angry. Just... he held it a bit longer than it needed to be.

Then a glance—one very direct look in Sim-Sim's direction.

I saw it.

He didn't say anything else. Just stepped back.

We've only been seeing each other a week. But we've already crossed that line—the one you don't step over lightly, not when you're my age and life's already thrown up enough drama to make you think twice.

It wasn't just sex. Not for me, anyway. I don't think for him either.

Now I've told him to hang back. Stay behind while I walk home with my ex and our son. Play the civilised card. Be patient.

And he agreed, but I felt the shift. Just a flicker.

And yet, here I am with Sim-Sim.

He walks next to me like it is not a big deal. With enough distance to give me space but still very much present. That kind of presence he can turn on like a light. The one that used to make people assume we were still solid, even when we weren't.

He's not hiding what he wants. The way he's showing up suddenly. Sticking close. Like he's waiting for a gap to open.

Jasper noticed.

Will he put up with it? All this... baggage?

Would I, if I were him?

SJ mumbles something about brushing his teeth. I nod, distracted.

"In you go," I say gently, nudging him towards the front door.

He trudges in without protest, pausing in the hall just long enough to glance back.

"Night, Dad."

"Night, mate," Sim-Sim says, warm but quiet.

SJ disappears. I hear the soft thud of his shoes hitting the wall, then nothing.

I stay by the door.

Sim-Sim lingers a second longer. His breath clouds in the porch light.

"I'm sorry I came," he says eventually. "Didn't mean to make things... weird."

I look at him. "Then why did you?"

He meets my eye. No dodging, no charming smile. "You know why."

I wait.

"Because I miss you," he says. "Like I said. I miss us."

"There hasn't been an *us* in a long time," I reply. "Not really. We were housemates with a joint calendar."

He nods, once. "I know. And that's on me. I let it happen. I stopped seeing what I had until it was gone."

I cross my arms. "It wasn't working."

"I see that now," he says. "I just wish I'd seen it sooner."

He doesn't push. Doesn't ask for anything. Just stands there, still and quiet.

Then he gives a small nod—half goodbye, half surrender.

"Night, Miranda."

He turns, walks down the drive without looking over his shoulder. The car beeps softly as he unlocks it. Driver's door opens. Closes. Headlights flare, and for a second the hedgerow lights up.

Then he pulls away, smooth and silent, tyres crunching over the gravel.

I stand there a few seconds longer, fingers cold, key still in my hand.

I shut the front door behind me and lean on it, eyes closed.

Why can things never be simple?

24

Snuggle Bells

Jasper

The lights are on in her flat.

I stand outside a little longer than I should, hand already half-raised to knock. From inside, there's movement—faint, quiet, domestic. The sound of someone loading a dishwasher or boiling a kettle. The kind of background you don't realise you've been missing until it starts to matter.

She told me to come by.

I nodded. Of course I want to come by. I've spent almost every night with her since our first official date.

But now I'm not sure if it still holds.

Her ex didn't just drop by. He fit. Knew the tone, the rhythm. Said hello to everyone like he'd never stopped being part of it. SJ lit up. Miranda didn't seem upset that he was there.

And I didn't have a reason to be annoyed. Except I was.

I'm not proud of that. But it is what it is.

We've been doing this, whatever *this* is, for a few weeks. We haven't spoken about it but there is enough between us that I don't like the feeling that I might be standing outside while someone else already has a key.

I knock. Two short taps.

She opens the door almost straight away. Same hoodie from earlier. Bare feet. No surprise on her face.

"You took your time," she says.

I shrug. "Didn't want to assume."

"You were invited."

I nod, but the hesitation's still there. "Wasn't sure if your ex would... change the invitation."

She doesn't answer.

Just steps forward and kisses me. No warning. No preamble. Just her mouth on mine—soft, steady, certain.

When she pulls back, she looks up at me like she's waiting to see if that's cleared things up.

And, fuck, yes it has.

She turns and walks back inside without another word. I follow.

Twinklesocks is sitting on the arm of the sofa, staring at me like she's been waiting for me. I reach out and scratch under her chin. She leans into it with a purr before giving my fingers a good lick.

"Charming," I mutter, giving her one last ear rub.

I head down the hall.

Miranda's already in the bedroom, back to me, switching on the small lamp beside the bed. Warm light spills over her shoulders. She pulls her hoodie off and lets it drop to the chair without a glance.

The door shuts with a faint click, before I cross the room and press my mouth to hers, one hand sliding into her hair, the other at her waist. She exhales against my cheek, fingers curling in the front of my jumper, holding tight, as if she's afraid I might pull away.

But I won't.

I can't.

The urgency between us is palpable, a quiet storm brewing just beneath the surface. We move together, our bodies pressing close, breaths shallow and synchronized. There's a restraint in our actions, a careful silence as we navigate the thin line between passion and discretion.

Her lips part beneath mine, inviting me deeper, and I follow, my tongue tracing the contours of her mouth with a tenderness that belies the hunger I feel.

Her taste is familiar, comforting, like coming home after too long away. I pull her closer, my hand at her waist sliding up to cup the curve of her shoulder, then down to the small of her back, mapping the contours of her body as if committing them to memory. She leans into me, her chest rising and falling against mine, her heartbeat a steady rhythm that mirrors my own.

"Jasper," she whispers, her voice barely audible, a breath more than a sound. It's a plea, a surrender, a name that feels like a secret between us. I respond without words, my lips moving to her jawline, then her neck, where I pause to press a kiss just below her ear. She shudders softly, her fingers tightening on my chest. The silence of the room amplifies every sound—the soft brush of fabric, the quiet hitch of her breath, the faint creak of the floorboards as we shift closer.

I step back just enough to pull my hoodie over my head, letting it join hers on the chair.

Her skin is warm beneath my fingertips, pale and luminous in the dim light. She's beautiful, not in the way magazines or movies define it, but in a way that feels real, tangible, alive. Her body type is a map of lived experiences—soft curves, subtle scars, a story written in flesh and bone. I trace the line of her collarbone with my thumb, then the swell of her breast, my touch deliberate but gentle, as if I'm afraid she might disappear if I press too hard.

"Quiet," she murmurs, her hand coming up to rest against my chest, as if to remind me of the need for discretion. But her eyes, dark and pleading, tell a different story. They beg for more, for everything, for the kind of intimacy that transcends words. I nod, a silent promise, and guide her back toward the bed. The mattress dips beneath us as we sit, then lie down, our bodies a tangle of limbs and whispered breaths.

The weight of her against me is grounding, a reminder of why we're here, why we do this. We're not just two bodies seeking pleasure; we're two souls seeking connection, a fleeting moment of escape from the chaos of the world outside.

My hand drifts down her side, over the curve of her hip, then lower, to the waistband of her jeans. She lifts her hips slightly, a silent invitation, and I undo the button with careful fingers, then the zip, my touch slow and deliberate.

I slide her jeans down her legs, her breath catching as my hand brushes against her thigh. Her underwear follows, left in a pool of fabric on the floor, and I pause to take her in, to let the sight of her sink into my memory. Her body is a landscape I could spend a lifetime exploring, every curve and hollow a testament to the woman she is—strong, resilient, breathtaking.

I shed my own clothes quickly, my movements urgent but quiet, and join her on the bed. The cool duvet cover brushes against my skin as I hover above her, my weight supported by my forearms. Her hands come up to rest on my shoulders, her touch both grounding and electrifying. I press a kiss to her sternum, then lower, my lips tracing a path down her stomach, my breath warm against her skin. She arches slightly, a soft gasp escaping her lips, and I smile against her, a silent acknowledgment of the power she holds over me.

"Jasper," she says again, her voice trembling, and I look up to meet her eyes. There's a question in her gaze, a fear of being too much, of asking for too much. I shake my head, my thumb brushing her cheekbone, and whisper, "You are perfect."

The words hang between us, a promise heavier than any vow. I kiss her again, slow and deep, our breaths mingling, our hearts beating in unison. My hand drifts lower, between her thighs, and I pause, my fingers hovering just above her, as if seeking permission. She nods, her eyes fluttering closed, and I press my palm to her, feeling the heat of her through my fingertips. She's already wet, her body responding to mine with a hunger that mirrors my own.

I slide a finger inside her, slow and steady, and she gasps, her hips tilting up to meet my touch. Her walls clench around me, tight and welcoming, and I add a second finger, then a third, my thumb brushing her clit in slow circles. She moans softly, her head tipping back, her breath coming in short, shallow gasps. I watch her, memorising every reaction, every sound, every movement, as if this moment might be our last.

She whispers my name again, her voice thick with need, and I lean down to kiss her, to swallow her sounds, to keep them safe within the quiet of the room. Her hands grip my shoulders, her nails digging in as her body begins to tense, her muscles coiling tight. I quicken my pace, my fingers moving in time with her breaths, and she shudders, her release silent but profound. Her body trembles beneath mine, her breath hitching as she comes apart in my arms.

I pull back slightly, my lips brushing her forehead, and she opens her eyes, her gaze soft and unguarded.

"You next," she murmurs, her hand reaching down to guide me to her. I shake my head, pressing a kiss to her lips.

"Later," I whisper. "Right now, I just want to be here, with you."

She rests her head against my chest, one leg slipping over mine, her fingers idly tracing along my ribs like she's drawing a map she doesn't quite realise she's making.

After a few minutes, her voice comes, low. "What are you thinking?"

I don't answer right away.

She shifts, propping her chin on my chest so she can see my face.

I meet her eyes. "Do you think there's still a chance for you and him?"

She giggles. "Is this your very calm way of trying to get rid of me?"

I don't smile.

The lightness in her expression fades. She exhales slowly and drops her gaze for a second before answering.

"I don't think so," she says, quiet. "I'm not holding out for anything. I'm not... waiting."

She pauses, fingers stilling.

"But he shows up, and for a second, I remember the version of him I wanted to believe in. The one who used to make SJ laugh in the middle of a supermarket. The one who didn't cheat. So yes, I get a bit confused. Not because I want him back. Just because it's strange to look at someone who used to be your whole life and realise you're not angry anymore. Just tired."

I nod, once. She watches me, like she's waiting for something.

"That alright?" she asks eventually, voice careful now.

"Yeah," I say. "It is."

I guess it has to be.

25

We Three Queens of Bluewater Are

Miranda

The toast is a bit too dark on one side, and the butter refuses to spread like a reasonable dairy product. I give up halfway through and let it clump where it wants.

SJ is sat at the table in his Spider-Man pyjamas, cross-legged on the chair, hair sticking up like he's been electrocuted in his sleep. He's already halfway through his cereal and deep into a dramatic retelling of a dream.

"Rexy had to cross this giant pit of lava, right, but the bridge was made of jelly. So he said, 'I'm not falling in that again,' and tied a parachute to his tail instead."

I nod. "Practical."

"He still crashed," SJ adds, shovelling a spoonful of cereal into his mouth. "But then all the other dinosaurs clapped, so it was fine."

"Good to know applause cures lava injuries," I say, dropping a piece of toast onto his plate. "Want jam?"

"Yes please. But not the weird one with seeds. That one gets stuck in my teeth."

I hand him the raspberry jam without pips.

We eat in the quiet rhythm of weekday mornings—chewing, mumbling, the occasional sound of milk sloshing and the soft thud of a dinosaur being repositioned beside the juice carton.

My tea is going cold. Again.

Jasper's mug from last night is still by the sink, rinsed and upside down. He left just after five, same as always—early enough that SJ doesn't notice, quiet enough that I only woke when I felt the blanket lift and the brush of lips on my shoulder.

SJ clears his throat in that very deliberate way kids do when they've decided the next thing they say is Important.

"Mum?"

"Mm?"

He picks at the crust of his toast, eyes not quite meeting mine. "Do you think you and Dad will get back together?"

I freeze. Not dramatically. Just long enough that the silence stretches into something noticeable.

I set my tea down.

"Where's that come from?"

He shrugs, still looking down at his plate. "You just seem to get on better now. Like when he came to the fair. You didn't look like you wanted to punch him."

"Well, I didn't *not* want to," I say lightly, but it doesn't land the way I mean it to.

He looks up.

I sigh. "I'm not mad at him all the time anymore, if that's what you mean."

SJ nods, like that makes sense. He folds a bit of crust into a rough dinosaur shape, then immediately bites its head off.

"Are you *going* to?" he asks, voice quiet now.

I pause, studying him. "Would you like that?"

He shrugs again. Less evasive this time, more unsure.

"I don't know," he says, picking at a crumb near his plate. "I like you like now."

I raise an eyebrow. "Like now?"

He nods. "You laugh more. And you don't do the thing with your face."

"What thing with my face?"

He screws up his own in a dramatic frown. "This."

I blink. "I don't look like that."

"You kind of did."

"Well, that's rude."

He grins.

I reach over and ruffle his hair, which he immediately tries to fix with all the indignation of someone who believes their fringe is a personality trait.

"You seem happier," he says, matter-of-fact, like it's just another observation. Like saying the cat's on the windowsill or the bin smells weird.

And I don't know what to say to that. So I just nod.

"Yeah," I say. "I think I am."

"But if you could be happy and with dad, then I'd like that too."

He pops the rest of his toast into his mouth and stands up, grabbing his dinosaur.

"I'm going to go brush my teeth," he announces, already halfway down the hall.

And just like that, the conversation's over.

But the echo of it lingers underneath the clatter of mugs and the creak of floorboards and the sound of Twinklesocks launching herself into the laundry basket like it insulted her.

You seem happier.

It's not a grand statement. Not a question.

But it's true.

Bluewater is heaving. Not sure what I expected when deciding to head to a shopping centre this close to Christmas.

"Right," Lizzie says, adjusting the oversized shopping bag on her shoulder like she's about to summit Everest, "if I don't sit down in the next five minutes, I'm going to start throwing a Lindt reindeer at strangers."

"You've already thrown one," I point out.

"Self-defence," she says breezily. "The man shoved me. Elbowed me out of the way for a diffuser that smells like pine and shit."

Amelia appears at my elbow holding what looks like three tubes of glittery bath cream and a single Christmas pudding-shaped dog toy.

"I don't even have a dog," she says, baffled. "Why am I holding this?"

"Capitalism," I offer.

"Peer pressure," Lizzie adds, sinking into a nearby bench with a groan. "And possibly early-onset festive madness."

I lower myself beside her and glance into my bag. Books, LEGO, a jumper for SJ that he'll hate and wear once for photos.

"Tell me again why we thought this would be fun?" I ask, pulling off my coat for the fifth time today.

"Because we were promised pretzels and festive drinks," Amelia says, scanning the horizon like a snack-deprived meerkat. "Also, I wanted to feel like a functioning adult with a list and a plan."

"And how's that going?"

"I've spent £83 on things I don't remember picking up, and I'm pretty sure I lost feeling in one foot around Marks & Spencer."

"Excellent," Lizzie mutters. "So we're all thriving."

There's a brief, collective sigh as we sit there, surrounded by bags and general yuletide chaos.

Then Amelia claps her hands once, startling a passing toddler. "Right. Costa. Stat. If I don't get some water and a hot chocolate in the next ten minutes I'm going to lie down on the escalator and let fate decide the rest."

Lizzie and I both grunt in agreement and haul ourselves upright with the weary grace of women who've survived total shopping mayhem. We gather our bags and make the slow, determined trudge toward the nearest Costa like three very glamorous pack mules.

Five minutes later, we're installed at a sticky table with cardboard cups, cinnamon dust, and a vague sense that we've earned this.

"So," Lizzie says, pulling the lid off her coffee and blowing steam across it. "Jasper."

I raise an eyebrow. "Subtle."

"Thank you," she says, deadpan. "Now talk."

Amelia leans in, eyes gleaming. "You've got that post-shag glow."

"I do not," I protest.

"You do," they say in unison.

I roll my eyes, trying to sip my latte like a woman with dignity, but Lizzie kicks my foot under the table.

"Out with it."

I pause.

I glance down at my coffee, then back up at them, cheeks starting to burn. "We've... spent the last couple of weeks together."

"Define 'together'," Amelia says, already grinning.

"Together-together," I admit.

Lizzie lets out a loud whoop that turns several heads, none of whom she notices or cares about. Amelia follows suit with a high-pitched "Yesss!" that could probably be heard from the John Lewis homeware department.

"Keep your voice down!" I hiss, laughing despite myself.

"Oh, absolutely not," Lizzie says. "This is the most exciting thing to happen since Bri hooked up with Omar."

"I swear to God, if you start asking for details—"

"We won't," Amelia promises, patting my hand solemnly. "Unless you offer them."

I bury my face in my coffee.

They both lean in, smug as anything.

I sigh into the lid. "Don't get that excited. It's not that straight forward as it sounds..."

Lizzie makes a weird noise and shuffles her chair a little closer.

I take a sip, stalling. "Sim-Sim turned up."

Both eyebrows go up in perfect synchrony.

"Mid shag?" Amelia snorts.

"At the Christmas fair," I clarify. "SJ invited him. I didn't know until he was just... there."

Amelia winces. "That's awkward."

"Mm."

"And Jasper?" Lizzie says, already guessing.

"Was incredibly polite about it," I say. "And completely calm. On the surface."

"And underneath?" Amelia asks.

I stir the coffee I've already half-finished. "He was jealous."

Lizzie grins. "Ooooh, possessive now, is he? I love it."

"I didn't say possessive," I counter. "I said jealous. Quietly. In that British, 'I'm-fine-but-also-I-might-die-inside' kind of way."

Amelia snorts. "Did he say anything?"

"Later. When we were back home, after SJ was asleep. He asked if I thought there was still a chance with Sim-Sim."

"Oh God," Lizzie groans. "Did you tell him absolutely not, that ship has sunk and is now an underwater museum?"

I laugh, but it's a little hollow. "I told him I don't think so. But I also said that when Sim-Sim turns up it messes with my head a bit. Because we had a whole life once. A messy, flawed, exhausting one... but it was still a life."

They're both quiet for a second. Amelia's expression softens. Lizzie, for once, doesn't fill the pause with a joke.

"And Jasper?" Amelia says.

"He heard me," I say. "Didn't storm out. Didn't sulk. Just stayed."

"Because he's a grown-up," Lizzie says, a little too smugly. "You're not dating a man-child. See how healthy this is?"

"I don't know if I'd call any of it healthy," I mutter. "But it's... different."

"And is 'different' good?" Amelia asks.

I glance down at my coffee again.

"SJ asked me if Sim-Sim and I will get back together because we don't fight that much. He said he'd like that." The words feel heavy, but I put them out there anyway, because I don't really know how else to handle them.

Amelia squeezes my hand. "He's not even nine. I'm not saying he doesn't understand anything, but for kids, relationships are black and white. If you don't fight, you must be good together."

"Exactly," Lizzie says, then narrows her eyes. "Oh god. You're not actually thinking about going back to Sim-Sim, are you?"

"And if she does, that's her choice," Amelia cuts in with a look sharp enough to make Lizzie wince.

"I don't know," I admit. "I mean, it's not just about me. I have to think about SJ too. But until I figure it out… how fair is this on Jasper?"

"Pish-posh," Lizzie waves me off. "Men do this kind of thing all the time."

"Yeah, and we don't like them for it," I sigh. "Anyway. Enough of my emotional turmoil."

Lizzie leans back and says, "Right. Finish your coffee, ladies. I need to find something wildly inappropriate for my boss before I lose the will to shop."

"Excellent," Amelia says, already standing. "I vote novelty wine stopper or 'world's okayest manager' mug."

And just like that, we're back in motion. Three women, too many bags, and one slight emotional breakthrough, promptly buried under sarcasm, caffeine, and questionable gift choices.

Business as usual.

26

Merry Feelings, Everyone

Jasper

Theo's coffeehouse smells like cake and hot chocolate.

He glides over with a plate of something flaky and delicious, sets it in front of me like he's presenting an offering, and says, "Eat. You look like you haven't had a proper meal since Tuesday."

"I've had toast," I say.

Geoff, already halfway through what might be his third piece of Gugelhupf, snorts. "Toast doesn't count. That's just warm bread with the consistence of cardboard."

I ignore both of them and stir my coffee. We're along the counter as usual. These bar stools are really only used by us.

"You're brooding," Theo observes. "Which means either a woman or the Christmas season is upsetting you."

"Could be both."

He sighs. "Right. Well, before you drag the atmosphere any further down, I'd like to share something truly harrowing."

Geoff perks up. "Does this involve blood or public humiliation?"

"Close," Theo says. "Lucy's nativity play."

I raise an eyebrow. "She's five."

"Exactly," he says darkly, as if that explains everything. "Five-year-olds in costume. Nothing but glitter glue and chaos. And somehow, I'm the villain for laughing."

"What happened?" I ask.

"Well. For starters, the sheep wouldn't stay in their positions. The innkeeper refused to give up his plastic chicken. And the kid playing the camel farted on the baby Jesus backstage."

"Strong start," Geoff mutters.

"But Lucy," Theo continues, pointing a finger like he's delivering a courtroom reveal, "Lucy decided to take control. Because apparently, 'Gabriel's not doing it properly.'"

"Wait—wasn't Lucy a snowflake?" I ask.

"She was *meant* to be a snowflake," Theo says. "But she came out wearing the wings from her fairy costume and announced—and I quote—'I am now Angel Queen Lucy and I know the story better.'"

I choke on my coffee.

"She then proceeded to narrate *the entire nativity* from memory. With added commentary."

Geoff's crying with laughter. "Please tell me this is on video."

"It is. But I've been warned not to share it unless Lucy is present because she wants to see people's reactions to her excellent performance."

"What did the teachers do?" I ask.

"Nothing. They froze. The headteacher was trying not to laugh. One of the shepherds was picking his nose aggressively throughout the entire performance and Mary dropped the doll when someone shouted 'SNACK TIME' from the back."

"Was the baby okay?" Geoff asks.

"Decapitated. Twice."

I rest my head on my hand, smiling. "And Lucy?"

"Proud as anything. Took a bow and demanded ice cream as a reward."

Geoff wipes his eyes. "I just love her."

Theo shrugs. "All I know is, next year I'm bringing a hip flask and low expectations."

I laugh quietly, and it feels good. Properly good. The kind of laugh you don't have to think about.

For a few minutes, I let the noise of the café settle around me. The hiss of the milk steamer. The clink of cutlery. The hum of people who aren't worrying about whether someone else's ex still has a foothold in the present.

Theo tops up my coffee without asking. Geoff leans back like he's just completed a triathlon made entirely of butter and caffeine.

"So," I say, before they can ask why I've been unusually quiet, "I've been seeing someone."

Theo freezes mid-sip. Geoff squints at me like I've just announced I've taken up interpretive dance.

"Define *seeing*," Geoff says.

"I'm dating someone," I clarify.

Theo sets his cup down very slowly, like he's worried sudden movement will scare me off. "You're dating. As in, willingly. With a human woman?"

"Yes."

"Not an alien or some high-concept ghost?"

"Still yes."

Geoff grins. "This is *excellent*. Who is she?"

"Her name's Miranda."

There's a brief silence, broken only by the clink of Geoff stealing another forkful of my pastry.

"She rents the annexe," I add.

Theo's eyebrows rise. "*Your* annexe?"

"Attached to my house, yes."

"Wow," Geoff says. "So not only are you dating, you've literally brought the relationship within stumbling distance."

"It's not like that," I say.

"Sure it isn't," Theo murmurs, sipping his coffee with the expression of a man who's heard denial before and isn't buying it today.

They wait. The silence is expectant, filled with the crunch of pastry and the sound of someone behind the counter frothing milk.

"She's divorced," I add eventually. "Has an eight-year-old son. SJ."

Geoff's eyebrows shoot up. "A child, too? Blimey. Straight in the deep end."

Theo watches me carefully. "And how's that going?"

I nod, a little too quickly. "Fine. Good. He's great."

But I know what I look like. Theo's reading me like a book. Geoff, slightly slower on the uptake, glances between us and narrows his eyes.

"You've got a face," he says.

"I always have a face."

"No, you've got *that* face. The one that means something's bothering you and you're pretending it's not."

Theo leans in, voice low. "You alright?"

I exhale through my nose and stare into my cup like it's going to offer wisdom.

"It's just..." I pause. "Her ex showed up. SJ's dad. Sim-Sim."

Geoff immediately sits up. "Sorry, his name is what now?"

"Not the point," I mutter.

Theo leans back. "Ah. *That* look on your face."

"Jealousy," Geoff says. "Classic. Bit retro."

I don't answer. Because it is that. Or something close to it. Something messier. Less dignified.

"I didn't expect to care this much," I admit quietly. "Not yet. But I do."

They don't laugh. For once, they don't tease.

Theo gives it a beat, then asks, "Are you worried she's still interested in him?"

I nod slowly, eyes fixed on the rim of my coffee cup. "I asked her."

"And?" Geoff prompts.

"She didn't say no," I say. "She said she *doesn't think so.*"

Theo winces. "Oof."

Geoff leans in. "That's... not great."

"I know."

"Technically honest," Theo offers. "But also, vague enough to give you hives."

"Exactly." I run a hand over my face. "She said she gets a bit thrown when he shows up. That she remembers things—the good bits, not the chaos. And she gets confused."

Geoff frowns. "That's fair, isn't it? I mean, if he's the father of her kid... it's always going to be complicated."

"I know it is," I say. "And I'm not asking her to pretend it's not. I just—" I stop. Shrug. "I'd rather know where I stand than keep wondering every time he turns up."

Theo folds his arms, studying me. "Do you think she's still in love with him?"

"I don't think so," I say. "But I can't quite tell if she's working through something, or just being careful. Or both."

Geoff nods, quieter now. "So what are you going to do?"

I pause, fiddling with the coffee spoon, scraping it gently against the inside of the cup. "I mean... I couldn't even blame her if she went back to him. They've got a whole life together. A son. That kind of history is hard to walk away from."

Geoff tilts his head. "But?"

"But I don't want to be the rebound. I don't want to be... the thing she does while she's figuring stuff out. I think I want to be more than that."

Theo says nothing, just watching me like he's already two steps ahead.

I glance between them, then sit back, exhaling hard. "I think I'm falling for her."

It lands in the quiet that follows.

Geoff blinks. "Sorry—say that again? I think I just hallucinated."

"I'm falling for her," I repeat, quieter now. "Properly. Not in the 'she's fit and we get along' way. In the 'I look at her and wonder where we are going to celebrate our ten-year anniversary."

Geoff stares at me like I've just grown a second head.

Theo, on the other hand, just smiles—not smug this time. Just... knowing.

"Well," he says, lifting his coffee cup in mock salute. "Welcome to the club."

"What club?"

"The poor sods who've fallen head over heels," he says. "I wrote Ivy a little love note this morning. You're in good company."

Geoff shakes his head. "You two are making me nauseous. I'm going to go flirt with the barista and pretend none of this happened."

He gets up and disappears in the direction of the counter, muttering something about emotional contagion.

Theo watches him go, then turns back to me. "You know what this means, don't you?"

"I'm doomed?"

"You're invested. Which means you'll have to stop hovering in the background like a Victorian ghost and actually tell her how you feel."

I grunt. "I was hoping there'd be a middle ground."

"There's not," he says, smiling into his cup. "It's terrifying. But also... worth it."

I nod slowly, the words still sitting heavy in my chest.

"I hope so!"

I turn into the drive, tyres crunching over gravel.

As the house comes into view, something shifts in my peripheral—a small shape on the steps outside the flat.

I park, engine ticking as it cools, and walk around the side.

SJ is sitting on the top step, hunched over in his hoodie, legs drawn up.

It's only when I'm closer that I spot Twinklesocks curled into the space between his arms. She's half-asleep, tail flicking lazily, chin resting against his chest like she's guarding him.

SJ doesn't move. Doesn't look up.

He's not crying, but there's a sniff, sharp and quick, and a swipe of his sleeve across his nose like he's hoping no one notices.

I step in closer and crouch beside the step, keeping my voice low and even.

"Hey," I say. "What happened?"

He shifts slightly, fingers still tangled in Twinklesocks' fur. His voice is quiet, flat around the edges.

"I got back from school. Mum texted she was stuck in traffic, so I let myself in with my key."

He pauses. Breathes.

"The cat gate was open and I didn't close the door fast enough. Twinklesocks shot past me and ran outside."

I nod slowly.

"I dropped my bag and stuff inside and closed the door so Thor wouldn't get out too." His eyes flick up, and back down again. "Then I ran after her. She nearly got to the side gate, but I caught her by the bins."

Twinklesocks shifts against him like she remembers none of it.

He looks back at the flat door.

"When I got here again… I realised my key and my phone were still on the side table. Right where I put them."

There's a long pause.

"I didn't know what to do," he adds, voice smaller now. "So I just waited."

His arms tighten around the cat. He's trying not to cry, and trying even harder not to look like he's trying not to cry.

I sit down on the step beside him.

"You did exactly the right thing," I say. "And you got the cat back. That's a win in my book."

I glance at the door, then back at him.

"How long have you been out here?"

SJ shrugs, eyes still down. "Don't know. What time is it now? I got here at four-ish."

Forty-five minutes. That lands harder than I expect.

"Alright," I say, pushing up from the step. "Let's get you inside. Come over to mine, we'll make some hot chocolate. And I've got the spare key."

He hesitates, arms still wrapped around Twinklesocks like she might do a runner the second he lets go.

"She can come too," I add.

He nods, quiet relief flickering across his face. Slowly, he gets to his feet, careful not to jostle the cat too much. She dangles in his arms like royalty.

I lead the way across the gravel to my front door, unlocking it quickly and holding it open for him.

"Watch your step," I say. "Shoes off if your socks are decent."

SJ snorts faintly—a barely-there laugh—and kicks off his trainers just inside the door.

Twinklesocks hops out of his arms and immediately stalks into the kitchen like she owns the place.

"Figures," I mutter.

SJ hovers near the doorway, rubbing his hands together. "Do you really have hot chocolate?"

I nod, heading for the cupboard. "The good kind. With the little marshmallows."

He doesn't say anything, but he sits at the table without needing to be asked. That, more than anything, tells me how rattled he was.

I flick the kettle on and pull out the spare key from the drawer beside the fridge.

"See?" I say, holding it up. "Landlord perks."

This time, he actually smiles. Just a little. But it sticks.

As the kettle starts to rumble, I pull out my phone and fire off a quick text to Miranda:

Me

SJ's locked himself out. He's at mine with Twinklesocks.

We're having a hot drink.

The reply comes a moment later.

Miranda

Thank you. Tell him I'm sorry.

I'll be stuck in traffic for at least another hour. Total gridlock.

I glance over at SJ. He's slumped at the table, watching Twinklesocks stalk the windowsill like she's patrolling her kingdom. His fingers drum lightly on the wood.

I tuck the phone away and drop two mugs onto the counter.

He watches me measure out the cocoa powder, eyes narrowing a little.

"Why do you even have hot chocolate?" he asks. "You don't look like a hot chocolate guy."

I glance over. "What do I look like, then?"

He shrugs. "More of a... black coffee kind of guy."

"Not wrong," I mutter, grabbing the mini marshmallows. "But I'll have you know I keep this in for Lucy." He gives me a knowing nod. "She thinks I make the best hot chocolate in the world," I say, tipping the marshmallows into his mug. "And then she told her dad he's only second-best, which didn't go down well, given he literally owns a coffee shop." I place a hot chocolate in front of SJ.

He lets out a small laugh and picks up his mug with both hands. Twinklesocks hops down from the windowsill and brushes against his leg as if checking she is still his favourite.

He takes a sip, then raises his eyebrows. "She's right," he says. "This is top-tier."

I lean back in my chair and give him a satisfied nod. "Tell everyone. I have a reputation to uphold."

SJ takes another sip, then glances around the kitchen—the way kids do when they're finally warming up again, curiosity returning in little flickers.

His gaze lands on the fridge. He leans sideways slightly, squinting.

"Is that meant to be a unicorn?"

I follow his line of sight to the drawing pinned with a magnet shaped like a baguette. Crayon lines, a lot of pink, something sparkly glued to the tail that's definitely not food-safe.

"Yep," I say. "That majestic beast is the work of Lucy. She insisted it was anatomically correct."

SJ snorts. "The legs are on backwards."

"She claims it's mid-gallop."

He stands up for a closer look, mug still in hand. "My mum would love that," he says.

I raise an eyebrow. "She's into unicorns?"

He nods. "Always has been. She used to have these unicorn slippers. Really fluffy ones. With gold horns."

I grin. "Sounds subtle."

"My dad hated them," he adds, smiling a little. "Said they were an offence to the eye. But she didn't care. Wore them all the time."

He pauses.

"Then one year we went on holiday, somewhere with a beach, and she forgot them at the hotel. She was properly sad about it. Even emailed the owners, but they'd already binned them."

He shrugs, then takes another sip of hot chocolate. "She never bought new ones. Said dad hated them so why replace them."

There's something quiet about his voice now. Not dramatic or heavy. Just the kind of quiet that comes when a memory catches you off guard.

I don't say anything. Just nod, and let the silence sit for a moment, easy and unhurried.

Twinklesocks hops up onto the windowsill again, letting us know she's had enough sentimentality for one evening.

SJ looks back at the unicorn drawing.

"She'd definitely like that one," he says. "Even with the backwards legs."

27

Rudolph the Red-flagged Ex

Miranda

The plates are in the dishwasher, the leftover pasta is cooling far too slowly on the side, and SJ is dramatically flopped across the sofa like he's just completed a marathon rather than eaten three helpings of dinner.

"Are you sure you're full?" I ask, folding the tea towel over the edge of the sink.

He groans into a cushion. "Too full. I might need to be carried to bed."

"You can text your legs and ask them to rejoin you," I say, dropping a kiss on the top of his head.

My phone buzzes on the counter.

I glance at the screen and sigh. "It's your dad," I say, reaching for it.

SJ lifts his head an inch. "Tell him I'm very full and I might be dying."

"Tell him yourself," I reply, tapping the screen to answer and flicking it onto speaker. "Hi, Sim-Sim—you're on speaker, just so you know."

"Oh. Hi. Hi, SJ," comes his voice, overly chipper.

SJ lifts his head just enough to speak, his voice full of theatrical drama. "Dad, I'm full. Like, dangerously full."

Sim-Sim laughs. "How many helpings?"

"Three," SJ says, groaning happily. "And garlic bread."

"Rookie mistake," Sim-Sim replies. "Always pace yourself when there's garlic bread involved."

"I regret nothing," SJ mumbles into the cushion.

"Spoken like a true champion," Sim-Sim says. "What was it, Mum's famous pasta?"

"Yep. The one with the crunchy bits on top."

"Ah, the good stuff. I miss that pasta. You're a lucky man."

SJ grins. "I know."

They both chuckle, and I find myself smiling too—watching them fall into that easy rhythm they always seem to manage when food and jokes are involved.

Sim-Sim clears his throat lightly. "So—the real reason I called—just wanted to check what time I should come and collect you both on the 23rd. And... Miranda, are you still coming for Christmas?"

Before I can even open my mouth, SJ bolts upright like he's been electrocuted.

"You're coming?! You're coming for Christmas?!"

His eyes are wide, delighted, hopeful in that pure, eight-year-old way that makes your heart twist and your guilt flare all at once.

"I—" I glance at the phone, then at SJ. "We haven't finalised anything yet—"

"Dad, she's coming, right?" SJ barrels on, already climbing off the sofa like he needs to start packing immediately. "You said she might, and now she *is*, right?!"

I glare at the phone. Or, more accurately, at Sim-Sim's voice.

"I said I'd ask," Sim-Sim says, all faux-innocent, like he didn't just lob a conversational grenade into my kitchen. "Thought it was worth checking."

I close my eyes briefly. I want to kick him. Just a light, satisfying shin tap.

"Miranda?" he prompts, all casual.

SJ is bouncing now. Actually bouncing. "Mum, please say yes! Granny does the Christmas crackers with the *socks*, remember? And the quiz! And the gingerbread decorating! And if you come, you can be on my team!"

I exhale slowly and pinch the bridge of my nose. "We'll talk about it later, sweetheart," I say gently, offering him a smile that feels a bit too tight.

"Okay," SJ says, still practically glowing. "But later can it be a yes?"

I ruffle his hair, steering him toward the hallway. "Go on, go brush your teeth and get your uniform sorted for tomorrow."

He calls our a cheerful "Bye, Dad, love you," and disappears into his room with a clatter.

I take the phone off speaker.

"What was that?"

A pause. "What?"

"You ambushed me."

Another pause, this one heavier. "It wasn't meant to be—"

"You told him I was coming. Before I said I was."

"Fuck! I'm sorry, Miranda, I wasn't thinking," he sighs.

I close my eyes. Maybe it really wasn't on purpose. "You know what SJ's like. If you say *maybe* with a smile in your voice, he hears *definitely* with Christmas glitter on top."

"I just... thought it'd be nice," he says, gentler now. "For him. For all of us."

I stare at the half-dried tea towel still looped over the sink. "I guess I am coming."

"Miranda, I can talk to him if you don't want to—"

"No. Let's do this," I say, voice quiet but firm. "Let's find out where we stand." Somehow it sounds like a warning, a threat, and not really like someone who is considering spending time with the other person.

He sighs. "Okay. Miranda, I really didn't mean to put you in this position."

Another silence.

"I... it's okay." I don't really sound like myself.

"Thank you," he says at last.

"Gotta go," I mutter. "Oh, and I am bringing the kittens." I need my emotional support animals.

"Miranda—"

"See you on the 23rd," I end the call.

Fuck! I take a deep breath. There is only one thing to do now.

"I'm just going to pop over to Jasper's for a sec," I call out to SJ.

He pops his head out of his room. "Why?"

"To say thank you. For the hot chocolate. And for rescuing you with the spare key."

He shrugs like it's no big deal—but there's a little smile tugging at the corner of his mouth. "It was good hot chocolate."

"I bet it was."

I slip my shoes back on and grab my cardigan from the hook.

"Five minutes," I say over my shoulder.

"Take your time," he calls after me, already half-wedged between two cushions with Thor curled on his feet like a smug, purring blanket.

I step out into the cool night air, the path between our doors familiar now—just a few strides, but somehow it feels longer today.

I should've texted. Or waited until morning. Or left it altogether.

But none of those things felt right, either.

He's been kind. Thoughtful. Patient with SJ. Better than I ever expected, and somehow that only makes it worse.

Because I can't string him along. Not when I don't know what I'm doing. Not when part of me still panics every time I see Sim-Sim's name on my phone.

Jasper deserves the truth. All of it. Not the polite version.

I reach the door and knock gently. It only takes a second.

He opens it in a T-shirt and jeans, barefoot, holding a book in one hand like I've interrupted something far too wholesome.

"Hey," he says, eyes flicking over me. "Come in."

I step inside, and the warmth of the house hits me like a wave. Familiar now. Comfortable. That makes what I have to do even harder.

Before I can say anything, he sets the book down, closes the door behind me, and leans in.

His hand cups the side of my face, thumb brushing just under my jaw, and then he kisses me—long, deep, like he's anchoring something. I kiss him back, because I don't know how not to.

But as I do, the thought breaks through—sharp and sudden:

This could be the last time.

And something in my chest aches with it.

I let the kiss linger longer than I should, even as my heart folds in on itself.

He pulls back slowly, his hand still warm against my cheek, and searches my face like he's trying to read a map with half the landmarks missing.

Then he steps aside, guiding me gently into the living room without a word.

The lamp in the corner casts everything in that soft, honey-coloured glow that always makes his house feel gentler than it should.

"I just wanted to say thank you," I start. "For helping SJ. And… the hot chocolate. He said it was really good."

Jasper leans against the doorframe, arms folded loosely across his chest.

"No problem," he says. But he doesn't look away.

He watches me for a second longer, then asks, voice low, "What did you really come over for?"

I take a breath. Then another. It doesn't help.

"I think…" My voice wobbles. I clear my throat and try again. "I think maybe we should just be friends… for now."

He doesn't flinch. Doesn't move. But something about the air in the room changes. Tighter, somehow.

I press on, the words coming quickly, like if I stop, I won't be able to start again.

"I don't know what I'm doing. With anything. And Sim-Sim, he's not who he was. He's different. Calmer. More involved. It's making me question things, and I don't want to lie to you about that."

Jasper doesn't say anything.

I keep going. "He told SJ I might come to Cornwall for Christmas. With them. And SJ got so excited. I just don't think I can take that away from him. Not if there's even the smallest chance it could work, for his sake." I pause, feeling the heat rise behind my eyes. "So I think I need to go. To figure it out. I don't know what I'll find, or how I'll feel. But I think I have to see."

Still, nothing from Jasper.

I shift on the sofa, wrapping my arms around myself. "I need you to know… it's not you. If this were just about me, if I didn't have SJ to think about, I'd pick you. I know you're the right choice."

That hangs there, heavy and awful. I look up.

"And I'm sorry," I add quietly. "I really, really am."

I stand, awkwardly, fumbling for something to say, something that will make this feel less like the worst idea I've ever had.

"I should go," I murmur.

I move toward the door, but he reaches out—not to stop me, not forceful—just a hand on my wrist, gentle.

"Wait."

I turn, and before I can say anything else, he pulls me into his arms.

He holds me close, one hand at the back of my neck, the other steady on my waist. I let myself fold into him, just for a moment. One last time.

"Thank you," he says quietly, his mouth close to my ear. "For being honest."

Then he kisses me. Deep, slow, no urgency. Just something that says *I'll remember this.*

When he pulls back, his forehead rests against mine.

"Take your time," he says. "I get it. Even if it kills me a bit."

I close my eyes, fighting back the tears.

"I'd rather you figure it out properly than stay with me and always wonder what if."

I try to speak, but there's nothing that won't sound like another apology.

He lets out a breath, almost a laugh.

"We can still be friends," he adds, stepping back enough to meet my eyes. "If that's all you've got to offer right now, I'll take it."

My throat tightens.

"And when Sim-Sim cocks it up again..." He shrugs. "I'll still be here."

I manage a shaky smile. "You're very confident."

"I've met him," he says dryly.

I let out a soft, broken laugh. Then I nod, and this time, when I leave, he lets me go.

28

Driving Home for Another Try

Miranda

The kitchen tiles are freezing under my feet. I flip the button on the kettle again. With Sim-Sim running late, there's enough time for another cup of tea. SJ is having a minor strop in his room that his dad is late, and frankly I'm pissed too. We were supposed to leave in the morning, but now we'll be lucky if we get to Cornwall by dinner time.

On the table, my phone is on speaker, mid-call with the usual group chaos.

"Wait, hang on," Bri says, her voice tinny with poor signal. "You're leaving today? Two days before Christmas?"

"Yes," I say, throwing a handful of toiletries into a zip bag. "Sim-Sim's picking us up in less than an hour. Please send sedatives."

"Why today already?" Fi asks. "Is Cornwall moving further away?"

"His mother's throwing one of her full-on Christmas Eve parties for the neighbours," I mutter, rooting through the drying rack for anything not still vaguely damp. "Apparently I'm now her honorary event assistant."

"Oh god," Amelia breathes. "Are there checklists?"

"There was a colour-coded spreadsheet."

A beat of silence.

"Right," Lizzie says, "so you're fleeing the village to play unpaid elf to your former mother-in-law. Absolutely normal behaviour."

I sigh, wrestling SJ's hoodie into the suitcase. "I know how it sounds."

"And Sim-Sim's collecting you?" Bri asks.

"I love Geraldine but she is not made to drive that far," I mutter.

It's easier to joke than to admit I haven't slept properly since the decision was taken from me. That I've replayed the last thing I said to Jasper too many times to count. That I nearly knocked on his door last night with a tin of Quality Street and no plan whatsoever.

But I didn't.

And now we're leaving.

"Are you sure you're okay?" Amelia asks gently.

I pause, then zip the suitcase shut with a little too much force.

"I just need to get through the packing. And the trip. And the part where I smile at people who once gave me a tea towel with *Mrs Sim-Sim* embroidered on it."

"Therapy," Fi mutters.

"Wine," Lizzie suggests.

"Or," Bri adds, "a last-minute detour to a certain someone's front door. A festive drop-in. Hot man, strong arms, unresolved feelings..."

"I don't have time," I say quickly, too quickly, reaching for my charger.

But it's a lie. I do have time. Ten minutes. Maybe fifteen. Just long enough to say Merry Christmas. Just long enough to see his face.

I glance at the phone. "You can say it, you know."

"Say what?" Bri replies innocently.

"That you don't think I should go with Sim-Sim."

"Miranda," Amelia says carefully, "we support you. Entirely. No matter what."

"Absolutely," Fi agrees. "Completely. Even if some of us... gently question your taste in Christmas transport arrangements."

There's a beat.

"I mean, you're not marrying him," Lizzie says finally. "It's a trip. To Cornwall. With your son."

"Exactly," Amelia jumps in. "You're doing this for SJ. And if nothing else, you'll get some fresh air and overpriced fudge out of it."

I shove a hoodie into the case. "I just wish I didn't feel so—"

"Guilty?" Bri offers.

"Conflicted?" Fi adds.

"Both," I say. "Plus chaotic. And mildly nauseous."

"You're a single mum packing for Christmas in Cornwall," Lizzie says. "Mild nausea is standard."

I collapse onto the edge of the bed, surrounded by half-zipped bags and emotional landmines.

"I don't know what I'm doing," I admit. "I don't know what I *want*."

"Then just go," Amelia says gently. "Go. Be with SJ. See how it feels."

"And if it doesn't feel right," Fi adds, "you come home early and we'll all pretend we never even had this conversation."

"Exactly," Bri says. "We're excellent at—" The doorbell cuts of the last of Bri's sentence.

"Oh, someone at the door. Sim-Sim might be early. Have a fab Christmas, you wonderful women! I'll text and see you next week!" I say quickly, grabbing my phone and hitting end as I slide, sock-footed, down the hallway.

A chorus of "Love you!" and "Don't die in Cornwall!" chimes out just before the call cuts.

I reach the door, still pulling my cardigan into place, and open it.

It's not Sim-Sim.

It's Jasper.

He stands on the step in a grey knitted jumper and tan cargo trousers, one hand tucked into his pocket, the other holding a medium sized, neatly wrapped box. The kind of box that makes you want to open it immediately.

He looks like he's stepped straight out of an outdoorsy winter catalogue, all casual handsomeness and light stubble. A complete clit-bait.

"Merry Christmas," he says in his deep voice that has more than once invaded my dreams.

"Oh," I breathe, surprised. "Merry Christmas. You look—" I stop myself before the word *ridiculously good* escapes. "—well."

He smiles, just a little. "You're all packed?"

"Mostly. Nearly. Ish." I step aside. "Do you want to come in?"

He glances past me, into the hallway. Then shakes his head.

"I'm on my way to the shops," he says. "Didn't want to interrupt. I just wasn't sure when you were leaving."

His gaze flicks down, and he holds out the box.

"I wanted to give you this."

I blink at it, stupidly.

"Oh. Jasper, I didn't— I haven't got you anything. I didn't think—"

He shakes his head. "It's fine. Really. It's nothing big. I just saw it and thought of you. And I wanted you to have it."

My hands curl around the wrapping paper almost reluctantly, like accepting it feels like a commitment to something I'm no longer sure I'm allowed to have.

"But," he adds gently, "you're not allowed to open it before Christmas Day. That's non-negotiable."

A smile tugs at my mouth despite the weight in my chest. "I can probably manage that."

"Good." His hands slip back into his trouser pockets. "That's all, really."

For a second, neither of us says anything. The air smells faintly of pine and the cinnamon candle I lit earlier. It's too quiet.

Then I manage, "Thank you."

His eyes hold mine for a beat longer than they should. "You're welcome."

We stand there for another second, the silence stretching just enough to feel fragile.

"Have a lovely Christmas," he says, and the ton of his voice gives me goosebumps.

"You too," I reply. "Really."

He nods once, then steps back off the mat, hands deep in his pockets again. I don't know what else to say, and he doesn't give me time to find it.

I close the door gently.

Lean against it for a second.

The gift is still in my hands, paper neat, corners folded just-so. I press it against my chest.

One tear slips down my cheek before I can blink it back.

Just the one. That's all I allow myself.

29

Good King Wenceslas Ordered Chips (and Whisky)

Jasper

The house is still when I get back from the corner shop. Proper still. Not peaceful, just… empty.

I shoulder the door closed and set the shopping bag on the kitchen counter. It contains a few questionable microwave meals, a multipack of beer that was on offer, and a bottle of single malt whisky I didn't technically need but wasn't about to leave behind.

The heating's on, but the place still feels cold. Or maybe that's just in my head.

I flick the kitchen light on. The bulb does its usual reluctant flicker before flooding the room with a glare that feels unnecessarily clinical.

I shove the beers and microwave meals in the fridge. The whisky stays on the counter. It's a decent one—picked it up more out of defiance than celebration. Something to make the place feel less bleak, maybe. Or maybe just something to toast the end of a weird year with.

I lean against the counter and glance around the kitchen.

Right. Enough of the pity party.

I reach for my phone and scroll to Geoff's number. He picks up on the second ring.

"Hey, little brother. If you are calling to moan about your non existing love life again, I tell you now, I'm not in the mood for once."

"Charming. When are you off to the rich wanker Christmas?"

"Tomorrow. Crack of dawn. I'm already regretting every decision that led me to this."

"Perfect," I say. "Come over. Early Christmas. I've got beer and a bottle of whisky too good to drink on my own."

He doesn't miss a beat. "Be there in an hour. Don't open the bottle until I'm there."

He hangs up before I can reply.

Pity Party for two coming up.

We've nearly finished the whole bottle of whisky, and I'm pretty sure I've absorbed half a kilo of melted cheddar through my bloodstream.

Geoff brought over two massive portions of cheesy chips—still warm when he arrived—and now the tray is littered with congealed leftovers and a fork stuck at a tragic angle like a shipwrecked sailor.

He's half collapsed in the armchair, legs sprawled, glass in hand. I'm on the sofa, stomach full, brain foggy, whisky glass resting on my jumper.

"She's gone to Cornwall," I say, for probably the third time.

Geoff raises an eyebrow. "You mentioned."

"With *him*."

"Still the ex, yeah?"

"Thought I'd remind you. In case the trauma wasn't properly set in."

He grunts, lifts his glass slightly. "Merry bloody Christmas."

We clink, barely. The sound is pathetic.

"She didn't want to string me along," I say, and the words come out all flat and familiar now. "Didn't think it was fair. Said she had to see what was what."

Geoff reaches over and pinches the last chip with any actual cheese left on it. "Very noble. Honest. Responsible. Still dumped you though, didn't she?"

"Appreciate the reminder."

He chews like it's a performance. "You think she'll come back?"

I stare at the ceiling. "I haven't got a clue."

"Fair."

We sit there for a bit, the kind of silence that only really happens between brothers or blokes too pissed to pretend anymore.

"I get it," I mutter eventually. "She's got SJ. She's got history. But..."

"But?"

I glance at him. "It still hurts like hell."

Geoff nods. "There it is."

I pick up the whisky bottle. It's got maybe a double left, if we're generous. I pour it into my glass and raise it in mock toast.

"To being the backup plan."

"To cheesy chips and poor decisions," Geoff replies.

We drink.

That's when the front door opens.

We both freeze like we've been caught doing something illegal. Technically, we haven't. Unless murdering a bottle of whisky counts.

Theo walks in, shutting the door behind him with the weary air of someone who knows exactly what sort of nonsense he's walking into and still hates it.

"Oi, oi!" Geoff calls, lifting his empty glass. "Look who's decided to slum it with the riff-raff!"

I grin. "The responsible sibling has arrived. We're saved."

Theo stares at us. "You're both drunk."

"Well observed," I say. "Detective Inspector Corbin, back on the case."

Geoff squints at him. "You're not even meant to be here. What time is your posh twat flight?"

"That would be *your* posh twat flight," Theo replies, pointing at Geoff. "I'm not flying anywhere."

"Tragic," Geoff mutters. "No wonder you're so grumpy."

Theo ignores him and heads straight for the kitchen, shaking his head as he passes.

"I got two texts," he calls over his shoulder. "One just said 'chips' with no context. The other was Jasper saying something about love being a slow death and asking what whisky monks would drink if monks drank whisky."

I grin into my glass. "Solid philosophical inquiry, that."

Theo reappears with two mugs in hand. "Ivy took one look and told me to go babysit my idiot brothers before one of them ends up in A&E and the other forgets he has a flight."

Geoff looks vaguely offended. "I'd never forget a flight."

"You literally just thought it was my flight. And can I remind you of the one time when you booked a city break to Vienna and went to Venice by accident."

"Different vibes, same vowel sounds," Geoff mutters.

I take the coffee Theo hands me. It smells like salvation and regret. "Cheers. Always good to be guilt-tripped into caffeination."

"You're welcome." He slumps down on the arm of the sofa. "I left a hot woman in my bed for this, by the way."

Geoff raises his mug. "A moment of silence for Theo's sex life, sacrificed on the altar of family dysfunction."

Theo rolls his eyes and mutters into his coffee, "Two drunken sods. Absolutely pathetic."

"Love you too," I say.

He takes another sip, looks at me over the rim of the mug like a disapproving therapist. "Right. When one of you is sober enough to string a sentence together, you can tell me what brought on the pity party."

Geoff points at me. "Him. He's the one with the tragic love life. I'm just here for the chips."

I groan and rub my hand over my face. "Fine. Short version."

Theo raises his eyebrows. "Is there a short version?"

"I'm attempting emotional brevity," I say, then nod toward the whisky bottle. "That was the warm-up act."

He waits, expression unreadable.

"She's gone to Cornwall," I say, slower now. "With her ex. For Christmas. To see if there's anything left worth salvaging, for SJ's sake. She told me she didn't want to keep seeing me while she was still figuring it out."

Theo's quiet for a moment before recapping my misery, "So... she ended things."

I nod. "Just for now, apparently. Though what that even means, I've no idea. Could be a month. Could be forever. I just—"

I stop, shrug.

"I didn't expect to care this much. Not this soon. But I do."

Geoff lets out a soft, sympathetic noise and mumbles, "He's a goner."

Theo leans back, exhales. "Alright. Now it makes sense why you were quoting whisky monks."

"I thought it was poetic," I mutter.

"It wasn't. It was deeply concerning."

I lift the coffee mug and take a long sip. It's hot and bitter and nowhere near strong enough to fix this.

Theo watches me for a moment longer. "And do you want her to come back?"

I look up. "Of course I do... but only if she wants to. Properly. Not just because it's easy or I'm nearby. I don't want to be the consolation prize."

Theo raises an eyebrow. "Did you tell her that?"

I nod, slowly. "Yeah. I told her to take her time. That I get it. Even if it's killing me. Said I'd rather she work it out properly than end up with me and always wonder what if."

There's a pause as both my brothers look at me like I've grown a second head.

Geoff blinks. "That's... wildly mature of you."

"Didn't feel it," I mutter into my coffee. "Felt like handing over a winning lottery ticket and saying, 'No, no, you go ahead and double check if you want something else first.'"

Theo leans back and stretches, still annoyingly composed. "Well, if it's meant to be, it'll happen."

Geoff and I both groan in unison.

"Oh, come off it," I say.

Geoff waves his mug in Theo's direction. "You've got a hot girlfriend who actually answers your texts. You're not allowed to go full Pinterest on us."

Theo smirks. "It's not Pinterest, it's perspective."

"It's smug," I reply.

Geoff points at him. "Exactly. He's hit the smug phase. Next, he'll be telling us 'Everything happens for a reason' and trying to make us do eat-pray-love shit."

Theo raises an eyebrow. "Alright, Shakespeare—have you thought about actually fighting for her?"

I blink at him. "What, like galloping into Cornwall on a horse? Shirt billowing? Bit of Heathcliff on the wild moors?"

Geoff perks up. "Can I be the stable boy who yells 'You'll never make it, Sir!' as you ride off into the mist?"

I ignore him and turn back to Theo. "This isn't a bloody Victorian novel. I told her how I feel. I was honest. I didn't play games. I've done the—" I wave vaguely, "—emotional transparency thing. Told her she mattered. Told her I wanted to be more than just a rebound."

Geoff coughs. "And you gave her the good loving."

"Exactly," I say, pointing at him. "Thank you. I gave her the good loving. Five stars. No complaints."

Theo grimaces. "Jeez."

"I'm just saying," I go on, "I'm not about to turn up in Cornwall with a handwritten letter and a glint in my eye. That's not romantic. That's emotional blackmail disguised as a Hallmark plot."

Geoff nods seriously. "Also, Cornwall's a four-hour drive... minimum. No one's that romantic."

I down the rest of my coffee and set the mug on the table. "If she wants me—really wants me—she knows where I am. I'm not chasing someone who needs space. That's not love. That's pressure."

Theo watches me for a second, then gives a slow nod. "Fair enough."

"And anyway," I add, flopping back onto the sofa, "if I ever do go full grand gesture, it'll be at least partly for the dramatic coat moment."

Geoff grins. "Can I come and hold the horse?"

"Absolutely not."

30

Feline Navidad

Miranda

The fairy lights are blinking wildly, making me wonder if I should warn people of seizure risk, the stereo is stuck on its third loop of Michael Bublé, and I've been handed no fewer than four different canapés I didn't ask for... three of which involved stilton.

The Christmas Eve party at my ex-mother-in-law's is in full swing.

All day, I've been chopping, stirring, fetching, folding, fluffing, plating. I've ironed napkins. *Napkins.* And while I was doing all that, Sim-Sim's mum talked non-stop about how happy she is to have "the family" together again. How lovely it is. How much Sim-Sim regrets his "little wobble."

Meanwhile, the men—SJ included—buggered off to do the "last-minute shop," which apparently involved an hour in John Lewis and then a three-hour pub lunch.

Now it's nearly eight, the heating is set to tropical rainforest, I'm in a party dress that's more ambitious than my mood, and I'm standing next to the buffet table trying to remember how to breathe whilst wearing Spanx.

"Miranda."

I glance up. Sim-Sim appears beside me, holding two glasses of Prosecco.

"You look beautiful," he says quietly, offering me one of the glasses. There is definitely longing in his voice. He is not just saying it.

"Thank you," I say, a bit too quickly, taking the glass from him. The fizz tickles my nose as I raise it, mostly for something to do with my hands. "I, um... can't decide what to eat. It's all a bit—" I gesture vaguely at the mountain of sausage rolls, cold salmon, and festive quiche, "—much."

Before he can reply, his mum swoops in like she's been waiting for a cue.

"Oh, salad's probably the safest," Irene says, plucking an olive off the buffet and popping it into her mouth. "You know how heavy Christmas Day can be, all that roast and pudding."

I nod, offering a polite smile. I already had some salad, actually.

"And now that things are looking up with Sim-Sim," she continues, voice low and conspiratorial, "you'll want to shift that little bit of Kummerspeck, hmm?"

She says it like it's an endearment. A cheerful pat on the arm follows. "Emotional eating weight," she adds, like I might not know what the word means. "Very common after a breakup. I read it in *Grazia*." Then she stalks off.

My mouth opens, then shuts.

Sim-Sim gives an awkward chuckle. "Oh, you know how she is."

Do I? Because she just called me emotionally bloated with a smile and a sprig of holly.

He turns to me, softening. "Anyway... thanks again for coming. Really. I'm glad you're here."

I offer him a tight smile. "Of course."

But something prickles—under my skin, under the party dress, under the carefully balanced good behaviour. Maybe it's the lights. Maybe it's the heat. Maybe it's the subtle way everyone keeps treating me like I've already come back, full circle, no questions asked.

I excuse myself before I say something regrettable. "I just need a moment. Back in a bit."

He nods, distracted by a cousin calling his name across the room.

Upstairs, the house is quieter. Still smells like potpourri and that expensive hand soap his mum keeps in ceramic dispensers shaped like geese.

I let myself into the guest room—the one she offered with great reluctance after I made it extremely clear I wouldn't be sharing with Sim-Sim.

The bedding is crisp. There's a Christmas-themed cushion that says *Let it Snow* in gold sequins. I sit down on the edge of the bed and exhale, finally, my fingers digging into the edge of the mattress.

I sit there for a while, smoothing down the front of my dress like that might somehow make it feel less tight, less deliberate.

Alright, yes. I've put on a little weight since the divorce. Wine and toast and occasional rage-baking will do that. But I'm still a size twelve, not that it should matter either way.

And yet.

The moment Irene said Kummerspeck, it was like a switch flipped. Like everything I've been holding together with politeness and seasonal cheer suddenly felt a bit flimsy.

I frown at my reflection in the wardrobe mirror. Still me. Still standing. Slightly shinier version, tonight. Lipstick, party dress, shoes I regret. But not unrecognisable.

Irene's comment shouldn't have got under my skin.

But maybe it wasn't just what she said.

Maybe it was the fact that Sim-Sim didn't say anything at all.

He just stood there. Sipped his drink. Carried on like it was normal, like it was fine, for his mother to imply I'd let myself go now that we were, apparently, back on track.

If he really liked me, really wanted this to work... shouldn't he have said something?

But then… I didn't say anything either, did I?

I just stood there, with my fizz and my frozen smile, and let the moment slide past like it didn't matter.

Maybe that's the problem.

Maybe it does.

The scream from downstairs pierces through the floorboards, followed by Irene's voice, sharp and echoing.

"Miranda!"

I'm already up and halfway to the door before the second shout.

When I reach the bottom of the stairs, the scene awaiting me could be from a middle-class sitcom with too much white wine. Irene is standing in the middle of the living room, jaw clenched, pointing at a horrified woman whose name I definitely should remember but don't. Said woman is holding her handbag at arm's length like it contains radioactive material.

"I told you to keep those cats in your bedroom," Irene snaps, her eyes narrowing on me like I've personally let loose a plague.

"I—sorry—what happened?" I stammer, looking between the handbag, the woman, and the suspiciously smug face of my eight-year-old, who's doubled over in silent hysterics.

The woman waves the bag. "That cat—that one—peed in it!"

I follow her glare and spot Twinklesocks staring back at me from inside the handbag like it is a litter tray. She blinks at me slowly, entirely unbothered. I mumble another apology and scoop her up, trying not to touch anything damp in the process.

SJ lets out an unhelpful snort-laugh behind me.

And then I see him.

Thor, belly to the floor under the buffet table, delicately nibbling what appears to be a stolen piece of roast chicken.

I close my eyes. Just for a second.

Then I scoop him up too, silently deciding I don't want to know how he got it.

"Sorry again," I murmur to the room at large, and make a swift, undignified exit back up the stairs, arms full of furry shame.

Back in the guest room, I shut the door with my foot and exhale.

Bringing the cats may not have been my finest decision.

The moment we're back in the room, both cats start purring like they've done absolutely nothing wrong.

Twinklesocks headbutts my arm, all innocence and fur, while Thor settles onto my feet like he's claimed the territory. I sigh, drop down onto the bed, and slide back until I'm resting against the pillow.

They climb straight onto my lap and make themselves comfortable. Within thirty seconds, they're both asleep. Purring. Dead weight. Warm. Unapologetic.

I am officially trapped. Emotionally and now physically.

I reach carefully for my phone, angling my arm around Twinklesocks' back paw, and open a new message to Jasper.

Me

You'll never believe what just happened. Twinklesocks peed in some posh woman's handbag and Thor stole chick-

> en from the buffet. My ex-MIL nearly combusted.

My thumb hovers over send.

It would be so easy. Just a small message. A funny one. No drama. No pressure. Just... a little connection.

But as I stare at the screen, the bubble of comfort starts to fade. *No, I can't do this to him*. I delete the message.

The screen goes blank. Quiet.

I set the phone down and lean my head back, listening to the rhythm of two sleeping cats and the muffled chaos still unfolding downstairs.

Still not my finest plan.

But at least they didn't knock over the tree. Yet.

31

Tidings of Unicorns

Miranda

Wrapping paper is everywhere. SJ's halfway through constructing a cardboard fort from the debris and has already declared this the best Christmas *ever*.

He's beaming at his new skateboard—bright red with lightning bolts and a helmet he insists he'll definitely wear. We'll see. I'm helping him peel one of those impossible plastic ties off a box when someone offers me a mince pie and a Bucks Fizz. I take both.

Around the room, there's the usual festive soundtrack: polite laughter, the crinkle of paper, a dad joke from Irene's brother. Christmas in full swing.

I'm just sitting back with my fizz when Sim-Sim hands me a box.

Small. Heavy. Too nicely wrapped.

"Oh," I say, caught off guard. "You didn't need to—"

"Go on," he says, smiling. "Open it."

I pull at the ribbon and lift the lid.

Inside is a delicate silver necklace—fine chain, sparkling pendant. Definitely expensive. Definitely a statement.

My stomach does that uneasy shift. I smile, automatically, but it's the kind that doesn't reach my eyes.

"It's beautiful," I say, carefully. "But..."

Sim-Sim leans in slightly, still smiling. "No buts. I wanted you to have it."

I glance around the room. All eyes aren't on me, but they *could* be in a second.

I lower my voice. "Sim... this is too much."

"It's Christmas," he says with a shrug. "It felt right."

I want to give it back. Tell him gently that this isn't where we are. That jewellery, especially jewellery like *this*, carries weight. Suggestion. Intention.

But I also don't want to turn Christmas Day into a scene. Not with SJ watching. Not with Irene looking like she's already mentally planning our vow renewals.

So I nod again. "Thank you."

I slip the box back into my lap and sip my drink.

My smile stays in place, but now it aches just a little.

A while later, the lounge has thinned out—people drifting towards the kitchen, the telly murmuring in the background. Sim-Sim's dad is already hovering near the wine like he's preparing for a tactical refill.

I glance over at the tangle of wrapping paper and rogue gift tags on the carpet. "Come on, love," I say to SJ. "Let's get your presents upstairs before someone breaks a hip."

He nods, gathering his skateboard under one arm and a pile of smaller boxes under the other.

As we head up the stairs, he says, "Can we give Twinklesocks and Thor their presents now?"

I smile. "Absolutely. Christmas is for everyone."

He speeds up with renewed purpose, calling, "They've been very good since we got them!"

"Thor ate someone's dinner yesterday. And Twinklesocks is a constant jail breaker."

"They are trying."

We reach the guest room, and the moment I open the door, Twinklesocks gives me a look like we're late for an appointment. Thor stretches luxuriously on the duvet, then flops onto his side as if he's not imprisoned but simply above it all.

SJ pulls two tiny stockings out of my suitcase. Each stocking is barely the size of my hand, stitched with glittery thread and crammed full of little cat toys—jingly mice, feather things, and what I *hope* is a catnip fish and not a novelty bath bomb.

We present them like royal offerings.

Thor pounces immediately, dragging one of the mice under the bed like he's hunted it himself. Twinklesocks sniffs hers with suspicion, then daintily pats a springy ball off the edge of the mattress.

SJ grins, delighted. "They love them."

"They're not repulsed. That's high praise, coming from Twinklesocks."

I watch them both for a second—my son, my chaos gremlins, the tiny stockings—and for a brief moment, it all feels strangely peaceful.

Even if there's a very expensive necklace in my hand and a growing weight in my chest that hasn't yet worked out what to do with itself.

While Thor murders a feather on a string and Twinklesocks glares at a festive jingle ball like it's offended her ancestors, I glance at SJ, who's now sitting cross-legged on the bed, fiddling with the empty stocking.

I clear my throat lightly. "You do know, sweetheart... me being here doesn't mean I'm getting back together with your dad."

He nods without looking up. "I know."

I wait a beat, watching him, the way his fingers twist the ribbon on one of the toys.

Then, after a pause, he says, quiet but clear, "I'm not sure I want you to."

That takes me by surprise.

I sit beside him. "No?"

He shakes his head slowly. "I like you in Kent. You're funny and chaotic. You don't make me iron napkins or do everything with matching cutlery."

A little laugh escapes me. "You never told me you noticed that."

He shrugs. "It's just different. You're different. In a good way."

I wait, because I can tell there's more.

"And here," he goes on, voice dipping, "you're not like that. You're quieter. You say sorry more. Yesterday you let Grandma say that weird word about your weight and you didn't even say anything."

My chest tightens. "I didn't think you heard that."

He shrugs again. "I did."

I look at him—my eight-year-old, who somehow always seems two steps ahead of me when I'm busy playing catch-up with myself.

"I think I like Kent Mum better," he says, and nudges the cat toy with his toe. "She laughs more."

I reach for him and pull him into a hug, tight and warm, his little arms coming around me without hesitation.

So do I, sweetheart. So do I.

It's late now. The house has quietened—just the occasional creak of ancient pipes and the hum of someone's overworked boiler.

SJ is finally asleep, curled up like a comma under the covers, one hand still loosely gripping a toy car he insisted needed to sleep "nearby for safety." I kissed his forehead, turned out the light, and stood there a little too long before slipping back to my room.

The necklace is now in the drawer and it's best off there. Instead, I go to my bag and take out Jasper's box.

I've thought about it since he gave it to me. Wondered what it could be, resisted the urge to peek, resisted the ache every time I thought about him handing it to me, standing there in his stupidly perfect jumper, smiling like it wasn't costing him anything.

I climb onto the bed, settle the box in my lap, and slowly peel away the paper.

Then I lift the lid.

And laugh.

Unicorn clog-style slippers. Fluffy. Ridiculous. White with little golden horns and pastel manes, like something plucked straight from a little girl's dream sequence.

They are... perfect.

Absurd, impractical, cosy—and perfect.

I spot the little card tucked inside the box, nestled between the slippers like it's trying to stay warm.

Dear Miranda,
A certain eight-year-old let it slip you once had a pair and left them on holiday. Thought it was time you had another. No princess should be without her unicorns.
love, Jasper

That does it. My throat tightens, and I let out a breath that's halfway between a laugh and something else entirely.

I slide my feet into them—soft, warm, immediately ridiculous. The manes tickle my ankles. They are not subtle footwear. They are joyful, ridiculous declarations of nonsense. And I love them.

Still smiling, I pad over to the dresser and open the top drawer.

The necklace is exactly where I left it, coiled in its velvet box, waiting to be something significant.

I bring it back to the bed and sit down. Stretch my legs out, slippers front and centre, unicorn horns pointed nobly at the wardrobe. I set the necklace beside them on the duvet.

One gift is chaos and colour. Laughter. Magic. The part of me that's messy and late and full of ideas. The part I'd started to rediscover.

The other is elegance. Weight. Stability. A future with edges smoothed and mapped out. A version of my life where things are done properly and no one forgets their salad fork.

I stare at both.

And for a long moment, I just sit. Slippers on my feet. Necklace glinting beside me.

Two lives. Two men.

And me, right in the middle.

32

Lonely Christmas

Jasper

The carpet smells faintly of pine needles and whatever festive candle Ivy's been trying to convert the air into since mid-November—something with cloves and orange peel and possibly witchcraft.

Lucy's nestled against my side, one bare foot resting on my thigh like she's claimed it, eyes wide as I try not to butcher the last page of *The Dinosaur Who Stole Christmas*.

I give the T-Rex a terrible growl and she giggles, exactly on cue. Job done.

Around us, the room is warm and slightly too full—wrapping paper stuffed into bags, coffee cups balancing on the arm of the sofa, someone's half-eaten mince pie abandoned on a napkin. The tree lights blink slowly, like they've also had too much food.

It's been a good Boxing Day. Too many roast potatoes. Too many terrible cracker jokes. Geoff phoning in from the States just long enough to show off the size of his hotel breakfast. Ivy fussing, Theo pretending not to enjoy it.

It's what Christmas is supposed to be.

And still.

There's a weight sitting just behind my ribs, refusing to shift. I check my phone again, subtly, like maybe I missed it.

Nothing.

No message. No "thanks for the gift." No photo of her feet in unicorn slippers. No emoji. Not even a Merry Christmas.

And I know what that means.

I close the book and set it gently beside Lucy's cushion. She yawns, then reaches for my hand.

"Can we read it again tomorrow?"

"When I am back next time," I say, brushing her hair off her face.

She closes her eyes. I stay a moment longer, pretending not to listen to the quiet disappointment humming in my chest.

Miranda didn't like it. Or worse—she liked it, and it only made things harder.

And she's probably with him. Sim-Sim. Perfect bloody timing Sim-Sim. What a ridiculous name for a grown man.

I push myself up off the floor, joints creaking like someone twice my age, and head to the kitchen to say goodbye and head home. There is some whisky waiting for me in my kitchen.

I find Ivy at the sink, elbow-deep in soapy water, sleeves rolled up, her reindeer apron declaring *Sleigh All Day* in glittery letters like it's an actual life philosophy. She's humming something jazzy and very much not carol-related.

"Thanks for everything," I say, leaning in to kiss her cheek. "The food was incredible."

She grins handing over a Tupperware container. "Thank your brother. The only thing I contributed was positive thoughts."

"Pretty sure I won't need to eat again until January," I try to object to the food offering that does look delicious.

"You say that now. Wait till you're elbow-deep in cold pigs in blankets at midnight," Ivy winks.

"Guilty," I admit. "Very on brand."

Theo appears in the doorway, mug in hand, watching me like I've just said I'm emigrating. He looks comfortable. Settled. The kind of settled I used to find a bit smug and now... I want it too.

"You sure you have to go?" he says. "Stay a bit longer. We've got that bottle of Brandy we didn't open yet and there's leftover trifle Lucy thinks she'll eat all on her own."

"She threatened me with a fork over it," Ivy calls out, without turning around.

I smile. "Tempting. But I think I need some time to myself."

Theo steps forward, brows knitting. "You alright?"

"Yeah," I say. "Don't worry."

He studies me for a beat, then gives a reluctant nod. "Text when you get in."

"Always."

I head for the hallway, pausing to glance back once. Lucy's still passed out on the floor under a fleecy throw, one of her slippers dangling from her toes. It's the kind of scene you wish you could bottle. *I love my family. So, shouldn't that be enough?*

I pull the door closed behind me, stepping out into the stillness.

The air's cold, fresh. My breath puffs in little clouds. I walk slowly to my car, hands in pockets, heading back to my own empty house where a bottle of whisky and a whole lot of me time is waiting.

When I get back at four, the house greets me like it always does. Quiet. A bit too tidy. The heating's kicked in, just enough to stop the chill from biting.

I head straight to the kitchen, still half in my coat. I place the little Tupperware tub Ivy handed me on the way out on the counter, the sticky label reading *Eat me. Or regret it.*

I pop the lid, and the smell hits me straight away—roasted, salty, deeply festive. I fish out a pig in a blanket, still cold but glorious, and eat it standing there like some sort of kitchen goblin. No regrets.

Then I reach for the whisky. No ice, no faffing. Just a good solid pour into the nearest clean glass.

I carry it through to the living room and drop onto the sofa with a sigh that belongs to someone older than me.

I raise my glass to no one in particular.

"Merry bloody Christmas."

There's a ring at the door just as I take my first sip.

Because of course there is.

I drag myself off the sofa, glass still warm in my hand, and head to the door. When I open it, Callum's standing there in his parka, cheeks pink from the cold and holding—naturally—a bottle of whisky like a festive peace treaty. Perfect, that should keep me going until the new year.

"Merry Christmas," he says, lifting it slightly.

"You're either the Ghost of Poor Decisions or a very welcome hallucination."

He grins. "Just me. Thought I'd swing by, make sure you haven't curled up in a ball of heartbreak and Quality Street wrappers."

I take the bottle from him and glance at the label. Good stuff. He always brings good stuff. "Tempting. Come in?"

He shakes his head, pulling his scarf tighter. "Can't stay. Stella's daughter's coming round in a bit. We're about to have a full-blown Christmas dinner."

"Ah yes. Nothing says seasonal bonding like stuffed turkey."

Callum smirks. "It's only the third one in the last four days. I'm starting to feel like a stuffed turkey myself."

I laugh, for real this time. It feels strange. Lighter than I expected.

He nods at the bottle. "I thought you might need that. You know, being brutally dumped just before Christmas and all."

"I wasn't dumped."

Callum raises an eyebrow.

"Okay," I concede. "Softly sidelined. Possibly benched."

"Exactly," he says. "And nothing says 'I'm processing this like a grown-up' quite like a nice helping of whisky."

"I'll drink to that."

He grins. "Merry Christmas, mate. You know where I am if you need someone to listen or mock you relentlessly. Both services available at no charge."

"I appreciate that."

He claps my shoulder, then heads off down the path, disappearing into the cold.

I turn to go back inside, bottle in hand—

"Jasper?"

The voice is quiet. Hesitant. But I'd know it anywhere.

I freeze.

Then turn slowly toward the annexe, heart doing something uncomfortable in my chest.

She's there. Leggings. Oversized hoodie. Hair slightly windswept. And on her feet—I swear I blink twice to make sure I'm not imagining it—are the bloody unicorn slippers.

Miranda steps forward a little, like she's not entirely sure she's allowed to be here.

"What are you doing here?" I ask, almost accusatory. "I thought you weren't back until tomorrow."

She shuffles forward, golden unicorn horns bobbing slightly with each step. Somehow, the ridiculousness of them just makes her look more like herself.

"I wasn't supposed to be," she says. "But I... made a decision. And I thought I should tell you in person."

My throat tightens.

"Alright," I manage. "Come in."

She follows me through the front door and into the warmth of the house. In the kitchen, we both gravitate to the island—it feels like a safe space. I set Callum's bottle on the counter, find two clean glasses, and pour.

We sit. The silence is steady, not strained.

I slide one glass across to her. She takes it, fingers brushing mine. Holds it for a moment without drinking.

Then she looks up at me, serious and steady.

No smile. No sparkle in her eyes. Not even the usual flicker of mischief.

And just like that, my stomach drops.

This is it. The final version. The "Let's be mature about this" conversation. No wonder she came in person—it's the clean break up talk, tied up with a bow and a dram of whisky.

I clear my throat and take a sip to brace myself. It burns a little going down. Appropriate.

She reaches across and lays her hand gently on my arm. Warm. Steady.

"Thank you," she says softly. "For the slippers."

I nod, not trusting myself to speak just yet.

"They helped me make a decision."

Ah. There it is. I look down at the glass in my hand, then back at her.

"They weren't supposed to be emotional blackmail," I say, too quickly. "They were just—"

"I know." She cuts in gently, fingers still resting on my sleeve. "I know. "What I meant was..." She lets out a slow breath. "They made me realise something. About what you see when you look at me. And what Sim-Sim sees."

My heart doesn't know which way to go—up or down, hope or dread.

I stay silent.

She doesn't move her hand from my arm. Just looks at me; not hesitant, not rehearsed. Just honest.

"Sim-Sim gave me a necklace," she says. "Expensive. Sparkly. Clearly designed to impress."

I say nothing. Not because I don't have things to say (I've got plenty), but because I can tell this isn't the bit where I speak.

"It felt like... like he was trying to buy me," she continues. "Or... I don't know. Win me. I don't think that's what he meant. Not really. He gave me what he thought I'd like. What he thought I should like."

She gives a small, sad smile.

"And that's what hit me. That after all this time, after everything we've been through... he doesn't actually know me. Not properly. Maybe he never did. And maybe that's on me. Because I never showed him. Not all of me. I never felt like I could."

Her fingers tighten slightly on my sleeve.

"But with you..." she exhales. "With you, I've been nothing but chaos. Half-together, half-unravelled, running late, forgetting things, having kittens as an accessory—"

"You make it look good," I mutter, mostly to stop myself from blurting something much more ridiculous.

She smiles, but it's still laced with something serious. "I've been myself, Jasper. Fully myself. And you never flinched. You never tried to change it or neaten it or hide it."

She glances down at the slippers, the pastel manes just visible below the kitchen island.

"You gave me the best present I've ever been given," she says, voice low now. "Because you saw me. And you wanted me to have something that made me feel like me."

She pauses, then adds, "When Sim-Sim saw them last night—when I went to talk to him, to tell him... he just said, 'Oh, must you wear those childish shoes?'"

Something tightens behind my ribs.

Miranda looks up again, gaze steady.

"That was when I knew," she says. "Really knew."

And I forget to breathe.

She slips off the bar stool without another word.

And then she's in front of me—close—stepping between my knees like it's the most natural thing in the world.

Her hands come up, soft and certain, cupping my face.

"Merry Christmas," she whispers.

And then she kisses me.

Deep. Certain. No hesitation, no half-measures. Just her, warm and real and entirely, impossibly her.

My hands find her waist without thinking, anchoring her to me like maybe I'm scared she'll vanish again if I let go.

But she doesn't.

She's here. With me.

In unicorn slippers. And chaos.

And she chose me.

33

This Christmas I Give You My Heart

Miranda

The kitchen feels suddenly smaller, the air thicker with anticipation. His dark eyes search mine, and for a moment, the world holds its breath. Then, with a swiftness that takes me by surprise, he closes the distance between us, his lips pressing firmly against mine. It's a kiss that says everything he can't yet put into words—a declaration of desire, of acceptance, of *us*.

His hands are on my waist, pulling me closer, and I feel the heat of his body through the thin fabric of my leggings. The kitchen island behind me is cool as he presses me against it, his kisses growing more urgent, more demanding. I wrap my arms around his neck, my fingers tangling in his dark hair, and surrender to the moment. The world beyond this kitchen ceases to exist; there's only Jasper, only this hunger that's been building between us since I declared us *just friends*.

"Miranda," he murmurs against my lips, his voice rough with need. "You're sure about this?"

I nod, though I know he can't see it. "More sure than I've ever been about anything."

His hands slide down my sides, his touch sending shivers down my spine. He steps back just enough to look at me, his gaze intense, searching. "Then let me show you how much I want this," he says, his voice low and husky.

Before I can respond, he's lifting me, his strong arms cradling me as he sets me down on the edge of the kitchen island. The cool granite beneath me contrasts sharply with the warmth of his body as he steps between my legs, his hands roaming over me with a hunger that mirrors my own. I feel exposed, vulnerable, yet utterly safe in his presence.

"You're so beautiful," he whispers, his lips brushing against my jawline, my neck, sending shivers down my spine. His hands move to the hem of my hoody, pushing it up slowly, deliberately, his touch both tender and possessive. I close my eyes, tilting my head back to give him better access, my breath coming in short, shallow gasps.

"Jasper," I murmur, my voice barely above a whisper. "Don't tease me today because I need you close... as close as you can get."

He looks up at me, his eyes dark with desire, and for a moment, he pauses, as if seeking permission. I reach up, cupping his face in my hands, and pull him back to me, my lips seeking his in a kiss that's desperate, needy. He gets the message.

With a growl of approval, he finishes pulling off the hoody and letting it fall to the floor. His hands move to my bra, his fingers deftly unhooking it and sliding the straps down my arms. I'm exposed to him now, my breasts bare, my nipples tight with anticipation. He lowers his head, his lips closing around one peak, his tongue swirling, teasing, and I arch my back, a soft moan escaping my lips.

"Fuck, you taste so good," he murmurs, his breath warm against my sensitive skin. His hands move to my leggings, pulling on it desperately. I lift my hips, helping him as he slides them down my legs. My unicorn slippers drop to the floor. My knickers come off at the same time as my leggings, leaving me completely bare to his gaze.

I feel heat creep up my cheeks, but there's no shame in this moment, only desire. Jasper's eyes rake over me, his expression hungry, appreciative. "You're best Christmas present ever," he says, his voice thick with want.

He steps back, just enough to shed his own clothes, and I drink in the sight of him—his broad shoulders, the defined muscles of his chest, the way the trail of dark hair leads to his erection. He's every bit as desirable as I remember, and my breath catches in my throat as he steps back toward me. The kitchen feels impossibly intimate now, the air heavy with the scent of our desire.

Jasper's hands move to my thighs, spreading them slightly as he steps closer, his erection pressing against my core. I reach down, my fingers tracing the length of him, and he hisses in a breath, his eyes closing briefly as if to savour the sensation.

"I need you," he says, his voice a rough whisper. "Now. But I need to get a cond—"

"Unless you are saying condiment—and I would have questions at that," I laugh. "—don't worry. I am on the pill."

"You sure?"

"I don't want there to be anything between us." Those words cause a groan to erupt from his lips.

There's no hesitation now, no more words needed. He positions himself at my entrance, his eyes locked on mine, and with one slow, deliberate thrust, he fills me.

I gasp at the sensation, my nails digging into his shoulders as he begins to move, his hips rocking against mine in a rhythm that's both urgent and tender. The kitchen island digs into my back, but I barely notice, too lost in the sensation of him, of us.

"Jasper," I breathe, my voice trembling. "Faster."

He obliges, his movements becoming more frantic, more desperate. The sound of our bodies meeting fills the kitchen, a primal rhythm that speaks to something deep within us both. I meet his thrusts, my hips lifting to greet him, my fingers tangling in his hair as I pull him down for a kiss that's hungry, possessive.

"I'm made for you," he groans against my lips, his voice hoarse with need. "And you are so perfect for me."

I don't respond, too lost in the sensation to form words. My body is coiled tight, every nerve ending singing with anticipation. Jasper's hands move to my hips, holding me steady as he drives into me, his movements relentless, unyielding.

"Come for me, Miranda," he commands, his voice a low growl. "Let me feel you."

His words are my undoing. My body shudders, my climax crashing over me like a wave, my cries echoing off the kitchen walls. Jasper follows, his own release tearing a guttural groan from his throat as he buries himself deep within me.

For a moment, we stay like that, our bodies still joined, our breaths coming in ragged gasps. Then, slowly, Jasper withdraws, his hands gentle as he helps me sit up. He leans his forehead against mine, our breaths mingling as we catch our breath.

"Are you okay?" he asks, his voice soft, concerned.

I nod, a smile playing on my lips. "More than okay."

He kisses me then, a tender, lingering kiss that speaks of promises and forever. Then he makes me link my legs behind his back. He lifts me like I weigh nothing and carries me, his semi-hard cock still buried in me, up to the bedroom.

Jasper

She's laughing breathlessly into my shoulder as I scoop her up, arms around her thighs, her legs wrap around my waist.

"Did we really just shag in the kitchen?" she murmurs.

"Blame yourself. You had to give me the best Christmas present ever. You."

She grins, soft and smug, cheek against my neck. "You're not complaining."

I am not. At all.

The hallway is dim as I carry her through, past the quiet living room. Upstairs, the bed's unmade but it doesn't matter. I set her down gently, and she immediately curls into me like she's meant to be there.

I wrap an arm around her, pull the blanket over us, and exhale.

It's quiet. Peaceful. So much so, I almost don't want to ruin it by speaking.

But I do.

"Where's SJ?" I ask, voice low in the dark.

She shifts slightly to look up at me. "With his dad tonight. They went to the game and now are probably watching *Home Alone 2*. Again."

I nod, my fingers brushing her back.

"And... how's he going to feel about this? Us."

She doesn't answer straight away. I feel her smile against my chest.

"He told me," she says, "that he prefers Kent Mum."

I blink. "Kent Mum?"

"Apparently, I'm funnier here. And more chaotic. His words."

I laugh quietly. Relief blooms, warm and unexpected. "He's not wrong."

"No," she agrees, settling closer. "But you like me this way."

"I don't like you."

She shifts slightly, tilting her head up, brows pulling together, lips parting—

"I think I love you."

The words fall out like they've been waiting at the back of my throat for weeks.

She doesn't speak right away.

Just looks at me.

And then that smile—the real one, the one that starts in her eyes and takes over everything—breaks across her face like morning light.

"Good," she whispers, eyes suddenly glassy. "Because I think I love you too."

And just like that, I'm gone all over again.

34

Auld Lang Sigh

Epilogue

Miranda

Ben and Amelia's living room is glowing: part fairy lights, part prosecco, part unhinged festive energy. The decorations are starting to sag, Coop's wearing a crown as if he rules over all of us, and someone left a wheel of Brie dangerously close to the edge of the coffee table. It's all very us.

To pass the time until midnight, we're playing *Two Truths and a Lie*, which has somehow turned into both a game and an informal background check.

Lizzie's turn.

"I once went on a date with a man who brought his own salad dressing," she announces, swirling her wine. "I was an extra in a

Wyclef Jean music video. And I can recite every single word of *Love Actually*."

Jasper, next to me on the sofa, raises an eyebrow. "Sorry—what?"

"She's serious," I whisper.

He blinks. "I—okay. That's... a strong opener."

Lizzie grins like a cat who once got a man to order kale with his own vinaigrette. "Lie detector time, folks."

"I want the music video to be true," Fi says.

"It feels true," Bri adds.

"The *Love Actually* one is definitely true," Amelia says. "She once did the airport scene in full."

"Look, I was performing," Lizzie protests.

Jasper looks around. "Is this a support group or a cult?"

"It's both," I say sweetly, nudging his knee with mine.

"The lie," Lizzie declares, "is the music video. Sadly. Although if Wyclef ever calls..."

Groans. Laughter. A round of "Of course it was the salad dressing guy!" and "You had terrible taste in men before Coop, Lizzie."

Jasper leans towards me, his arm brushing mine. "I am both terrified and fascinated by your friends."

"You'll get used to it."

He gives me a sideways look. "Will I survive it?"

"If the gay porn didn't scare you off, nothing will."

He grins. "Fair point."

A few rounds later, it's my turn. The room quiets down in that way it does when people think you're going to embarrass yourself and they want front-row seats.

I clear my throat. "Okay. One: I once got stuck in a changing room trying to take off a sports bra. Two: I nearly threw up on Prince Harry. Three: I just bought unicorn underwear."

Jasper glances at me. "Oh no."

"Oh yes."

Fi sighs. "These are *all* true. I'm sure of it."

"That's not how the game works," George points out.

"Miranda doesn't play by the rules," Bri says, fondly.

Amelia raises her glass. "To chaos in human form."

"Oi," I protest, laughing. "There's one lie in there, thank you very much."

Before anyone can guess, Ben comes in with the bottle of prosecco. "Five minutes, folks!"

Jasper leans in and nudges me gently. "Should we wake SJ?"

I glance over at the sofa, where he's curled up next to Robbie, Fi's son, both of them in a tangle of blankets and popcorn debris, mouths slightly open, limbs flopped in the pure drama of deep child-sleep.

"If we don't," I murmur, "we'll never hear the end of it. He's been banging on about staying up till midnight for weeks. He'd disown me."

Jasper gives a solemn nod. "Right. Parental survival strategy. Let's do it."

Fi and I cross the room, Fi going for Robbie while I crouch beside SJ and gently nudge his shoulder.

"Sweetheart," I whisper. "Come on. Five minutes till midnight."

He stirs, groggy and confused. "Is it New Year yet?"

"Almost. Come on. Coats on. Fireworks incoming."

Fi gently wakes Robbie, who responds by sitting bolt upright and declaring he was "just resting his eyes."

A flurry of jackets and borrowed scarves follows, everyone suddenly piling into the hallway, a gaggle of sleepy children and tipsy adults wrapped in wool and excitement.

Ben opens the back doors with a theatrical flourish. "To the field we go!"

We pour out into the garden, laughter chasing our steps, and trudge through the crisp night. The sky's clear, a scattering of stars overhead, the kind that only appear when you're away from the city and close to midnight.

Out past the garden hedge, the field slopes gently down, giving us a perfect view over the villages below. Dotted lights, silhouettes of rooftops, and somewhere, faint music drifting on the air from another party.

Coop hands the boys their sparklers like he's officiating a sacred ritual. SJ and Robbie don't even wait for instruction—they're already racing around the garden, shrieking with laughter, drawing flaming figure eights in the cold air.

"Don't run with fire!" Amelia calls, half-laughing.

"They're fine," Coop says confidently. "I gave them a safety chat."

"What did that involve?" Bri asks.

"Mostly the advice to have fun."

The rest of us gather at the edge of the garden. The countdown begins, slightly off-beat and very enthusiastic.

"Ten! Nine! Eight!"

I feel Jasper shift beside me. His hand slides into mine, warm and steady. I glance up. He's already looking at me.

"Seven! Six!"

SJ is a blur of sparkler-light and laughter in the background, a comet in mittens.

"Five! Four!"

Jasper steps in closer, his other hand finding my waist.

"Three! Two!"

The noise around us starts to blur.

"One—"

Midnight.

I turn into his arms just as he kisses me. Soft. Slow. Certain.

The sparkler light flickers against his jaw, and the cold barely registers with the heat of his mouth on mine.

When he pulls back, his voice is low—just for me.

"I didn't think my year would end with you."

I blink up at him, heart thudding stupidly hard.

"But from now on," he says, brushing his thumb along my cheek, "I want every year to start and end with you."

There it is—that lump in my throat again. That stupid, perfect ache.

"Then you'd better stick around, Corbin," I whisper.

He smiles—wide and open and all in.

"I'm not going anywhere, Princess."

This was the last book in the Cat Ladies Rule the World Series. Do you want more? Keep an eye out for the series bundle (release in December) It will feature an exclusive interview with our cat ladies (and their men) as they spill the beans on cats, love and what comes next.

The Corbin Brothers will be back in 2026 in

The Bedroom Ban – Finding Myself... One Awkward Date at a Time.

Psst... here's a little secret. The Corbins aren't done with Christmas Chaos just yet! In 2026 we'll be heading to Guernsey for another festive adventure.

More details will be unwrapped on 13 December 2025.

MORE FROM

Dani Elias

More from Dani Elias

Mind the Corbin Brothers

The Dating Ban – Finding myself… one clay gnome at a time

The Bedroom Ban: Finding myself… one awkward date at a time

Aftermath

Mission

Escape

Rescue

Cat Ladies Rule The World

Valentine's Rebellion (Prequel Novella)

The Unnatural Habitat of a Cat Lady

The Unconventional Journey of a Cat Lady

The Unhinged Christmas of a Cat Lady

Greenview Manor Tales

Fierce Family

Alluring Adventure

Elusive Embrace

Wistful Whispers

Spellbinding Spirit

Fellside Mountain Rescue Series

Currently being updated. Will be available again in 2026

The Ramblers of St Claire

Twisted Paths

Crossed Paths

Fated Paths

Standalone

Christmas Alibi

Surprise Me Tonight

Printed in Dunstable, United Kingdom

70021812R00203